Green Glitter Girl

green glitter girl

Connie C. Jones, M.A., L.P.C.
with Melanie Davis-Jones

Vista, CA

Copyright © 2025 by Connie C. Jones

All rights reserved. Torchflame Books supports copyright. Copyright fuels creativity, encourages diverse voices, promotes free speech, and creates a vibrant culture. Thank you for buying an authorized edition of this book and for complying with copyright laws by not reproducing, scanning, or distributing any part of it in any form without permission, except by a reviewer who wishes to quote brief passages in connection with a review written for insertion in a magazine, newspaper, broadcast, website, blog or other outlet. You are supporting independent publishing and allowing Torchflame Books to publish books for all readers.

NO AI TRAINING: Without in any way limiting the author's [and publisher's] exclusive rights under copyright, any use of this publication to "train" generative artificial intelligence (AI) technologies to generate text is expressly prohibited. The author reserves all rights to license uses of this work for generative AI training and development of machine learning language models.

ISBN: 978-1-61153-610-2 (paperback)

ISBN: 978-1-61153-611-9 (ebook)

ISBN: 978-1-61153-612-6 (large print)

Library of Congress Control Number: 2025919173

Green Glitter Girl is published by: Torchflame Books, an imprint of Top Reads Publishing, LLC, 1035 E. Vista Way, Suite 205, Vista, CA 92084, USA

Permissions Pending

Cover design and interior layout: Jori Hanna

The publisher is not responsible for websites or social media accounts (or their content) that are not owned by the publisher.

*Dedicated to the Lifegiver
To the Spirit within each of us that, if chosen,
will enable us to reconnect to our
True Selves and to rise from the
ashes like the phoenix*

This memoir contains reflections on real events and personal experiences, including themes of trauma, abuse, loss, and recovery. The author has recounted her truth as faithfully as memory allows. Some content may be distressing to readers.

Discretion is advised, particularly for those who may be navigating similar experiences. The intention of this memoir is to bear witness to the complex realities that shape a life, the healing power of the body, and the resilience of the human spirit.

Foreword by Stephen Porges, PhD

At its core, *Green Glitter Girl* is more than a memoir—it is a testament to the power of the human nervous system to adapt, survive, and ultimately heal. It is a story that vividly illustrates the neurophysiological processes underlying trauma and resilience, aligning with the principles of Polyvagal Theory. As a scientist who has spent decades studying the nervous system's response to safety and danger, I see in this book not just a personal account, but a lived example of the transformative process of healing.

I have had the privilege of meeting the author and discussing her trauma history and heroic adaptive journey. Her story is one of profound courage, demonstrating the extraordinary capacity of the nervous system to protect, endure, and ultimately to heal. Through our discussions, I have witnessed how her adaptive strategies align with Polyvagal Theory—how she has learned to regulate her nervous system, reframe past experiences, and move from a state of survival to one of thriving. Her experiences reflect the very essence of Polyvagal Theory—how our autonomic nervous system continuously navigates between states of safety, mobilization, and shutdown in response to life's challenges.

Polyvagal Theory, which I first introduced in the 1990s, provides a framework for understanding how our autonomic nervous system shapes our experiences, particularly in the face of trauma. The autonomic nervous system is not just a background regulator of bodily functions; it is central to how we engage with the world, how we form relationships, and how we recover from adversity. Our nervous system operates through three primary states: the ventral vagal system, which fosters social engagement and safety; the sympathetic system, which mobilizes us for fight or flight in response to perceived danger; and the dorsal vagal system, which, when activated in an overwhelming context, leads to shutdown, dissociation, or immobilization. These states are not choices we make consciously but are rather automatic responses to the world around us, shaped by our early experiences.

In *Green Glitter Girl*, we see how early trauma can disrupt these natural patterns of regulation. The author's childhood experiences—marked by loss, neglect, and profound stress—reveal a nervous system in constant survival mode, oscillating between hypervigilance and collapse. In moments of extreme distress, such as the loss of her beloved sister and the emotional neglect of her caregivers, the autonomic nervous system likely defaulted to a state of immobilization. When a child is left without the support of a responsive, attuned caregiver, the nervous system adapts in the only way it can: It shuts down to protect itself. This is not weakness, nor is it pathology; it is biology. It is the body's profound attempt at self-preservation.

Yet what makes this story so powerful is not just the depiction of trauma, but the demonstration of healing. Polyvagal Theory teaches us that recovery is not a purely cognitive process; it is deeply physiological. Healing occurs when the nervous system can reestablish a sense of safety, when the body can learn to move out of defense and into connection. *Green Glitter Girl* illustrates this journey beautifully, showing how the process of reclaiming one's voice and sense of self is not about simply "getting over" trauma, but about finding ways to reenter a state of safety and connection.

A key component of this healing journey is what I call "neuroception"—the nervous system's ability to detect cues of safety or danger below the level of conscious awareness. For individuals who have experienced profound early trauma, the neuroceptive system is often tuned toward threat, meaning even neutral or positive experiences can feel unsafe. The work of healing, then, involves reshaping this system, creating new patterns of detection, interoception, perception, and response that allow for a greater sense of security in relationships and in the body itself.

In the author's journey, we see the importance of

embodied healing practices—those that engage the body as an active participant in the recovery process. Whether through physical movement, somatic therapy, breathwork, or safe social connection, these approaches help shift the nervous system out of chronic defense and into a state where true healing can occur. *Green Glitter Girl* offers us a powerful narrative of this shift, showing how trauma can be processed not just through words, but through the body's own capacity to find safety again.

Another vital lesson in this book is the role of co-regulation in healing. As humans, we are wired for connection. The nervous system does not regulate itself in isolation; it requires the presence of safe, attuned others to help shape its responses. This is why early attachment relationships are so critical in setting the stage for lifelong emotional regulation. When those early relationships are unsafe or absent, healing later in life often requires new, reparative relationships that offer the co-regulation that was previously missing. The moments of connection the author experiences throughout her journey—whether with compassionate mentors, friends, or, later, with the individuals she helps in her own work—are examples of this process in action.

Importantly, *Green Glitter Girl* also sheds light on the cultural and social dimensions of trauma. The stigma around discussing trauma, the societal pressures to "move on," and the misunderstanding of dissociation and survival responses can all contribute to the isolation many survivors feel. Societal expectations can shape an individual's nervous system responses, making it harder to access healing pathways. Understanding these influences allows us to challenge narratives that discourage emotional expression and create spaces where healing is truly possible. The courage in telling this story helps break that silence, offering a beacon of understanding for others who may be navigating similar paths.

As you read this book, I encourage you to do so with an awareness of your own physiological responses. Notice how your body reacts to different parts of the story. Do you feel tension, a quickening of your breath, or a sense of unease? Or do you find moments where you feel warmth, connection, or relief? These reactions are important. They are your nervous system's way of engaging with the narrative, mirroring the same processes that shape our daily interactions and sense of self.

The journey outlined in these pages is one of profound transformation. One particularly striking moment in the book that illustrates this shift is when the author first experiences a sense of safety in connection with another person after years of isolation. That moment—a turning point in her nervous system's recalibration—demonstrates the power of co-regulation in restoring a sense of self and belonging. It is a movement from survival to safety, from disconnection to connection, from silence to voice. It embodies the principles of Polyvagal Theory not in abstract terms, but in lived experience, demonstrating that healing is possible when we understand and work with our nervous system rather than against it.

I am honored to write this foreword, not just as a scientist, but as someone who believes in the possibility of healing for all who have endured trauma. *Green Glitter Girl* is a gift—one that reminds us that no matter how deep the wounds, the body and mind have an extraordinary capacity to heal. May this book serve as an invitation to explore your own journey with compassion, and may it be a source of hope for those who seek to reclaim their sense of self and safety in the world.

Stephen Porges, PhD
Creator of Polyvagal Theory
Distinguished University Scientist, Kinsey Institute
Indiana University

Introduction

Unresolved trauma diminishes a life and may even destroy it. However, trauma does not have to dictate the outcome of your life. It is not possible to live life and avoid trauma entirely in this world. But it is possible to acknowledge trauma, embrace its effects, and begin the journey of healing and recovering the life that is your own.

I was traumatized as a child and spent many years frozen in that trauma, unable to realize my true self, but now I have meaningful work; I have people who unconditionally love me; I have true joy; and I have recovered myself and my soul. I have reconnected "to a vital animating core of our embodied selves—a certain essential something that links us (through love) to the divine, to each other, and to the exquisite beauties of the natural and cultural world. We know the soul when we experience it," Donald Kalsched says in *Trauma and the Soul*.

What I know is the same process that brought me here—to healing—is available to you. This book is my story, written in the hope that it will help you reconnect to yourself too.

Hope

I was born into a sorrowful house. It was sorrowful because it was home to two parents who were profoundly depressed and two older brothers, one of whom was a molester. My father, the doctor, could not pay enough attention to offer his family the care they needed. My mother lashed out at those around her and crushed them to her will. I didn't know what a sorrowful house it was at first. I was too little. I knew only that I was terrified much of the time. Strange things happened. My oldest brother would come into my room at night and fondle me. No child could manage the resultant feelings; the resources simply were not there. I'd lie awake in bed at night waiting, terrified, for the doorknob to turn. When daylight came, it was no better. My mother's rage would flatten me. I tried to fix her, to make her better, to be a good girl, but nothing worked. I couldn't eat, I couldn't sleep, and sometimes I couldn't even breathe. Most importantly, I couldn't speak. Silence was the rule. Nobody talked about what was really going on in that house. It was forbidden without anyone even having to say that was our way.

The house was built for the town's revered Dr. Robert Cummins. It was a gray square frame structure of deliberate blandness, like those houses that burst open in the news to reveal the horrors that have taken place inside. (Some neighbor always says, "They seemed so normal . . .") That doctor was my father. I believe he loved me. But he was frozen in his own paralyzing depression; he could not reach through the dense wall. My mother had been so disturbed in her own childhood that she could not love. She could only rage.

Then one day into this dark and frightening place came a shining light. Looking back from the point of view of adulthood, I have no idea how that shattered couple achieved this, but a sweet baby came into our house. She was bright and pink and beautiful, and I saw at once that she could be my salvation, my escape from this horrifying house where I found myself trapped. Elizabeth Ann was her name. Betsy, we called her. I knew I would tend to her and nurture her—we would be inseparable and stand by each other forever, protecting each other from the forces of the twisted world.

I was just a toddler when Betsy was born, but I loved my sister as I had never loved anyone. She was a free spirit, unsullied by the contamination of the house. I recognized in her a human quality that was missing from my family. She loved. She gazed. She lived. She sparkled. She was pure light. For perhaps the first time, I was happy, and it was all about Betsy.

As Betsy grew and began to crawl and then say words, I was thrilled at the idea that I had at last found the companion I had been seeking all my young life. I was not alone any longer. This child was meant to become my friend and companion in facing a terrifying world. Betsy learned to walk, and we became inseparable, tumbling together like kittens, laughing and giggling in our secret bond against the night. I knew things that Betsy did not yet know, like how dangerous nighttime and this world could be. I knew I would have to teach Betsy and take care of her as a big sister should, but for now we had her innocence, and we had each other; our bond was unbreakable.

Although I was only three, I knew a lot already. Terrifying undercurrents ran through my family, and even at that age, I could read them in that torrent of nonverbal information that constantly flows around us through the natural world. I was afraid of my mom, and I think that is why my sister held such hope for me. She was going to be my partner. She was just a little too young to teach quite yet. I had to bide my time, but we would grow up and be together forever.

It was May Day in a small town on the Fox River in Illinois. An icy rain stung our faces as we left the warmth of the car and walked out across a manicured lawn. Lines of grave markers stretched away into the mist. Boughs of ancient evergreens, bending low in the wind, cast off lobes of water like strings of pearls. I walked with my husband Harry across the grass to the two gray gravestones, thin as playing cards among the other monuments. Each slab of slate was set in a pediment of colorless concrete. The only differences between the two were the names and dates and the emblem etched above that information. C. Robert Cummins, the town doctor. His life began on May 31, 1922, and ended on March 12, 1969. A cluster of grapes was engraved at the top of his headstone. His daughter, Elizabeth Ann, lay beside him. Betsy. She lived from April 15, 1955, to September 19, 1956. Her gravestone bore a dove in flight.

My mother, Joan Marguerite Sill, anglicized from the Polish "Cylkowski," was conspicuously absent from the scene. She wanted to be buried in St. Louis where she had lived the final years of her life. It was an odd scene, the baby's marker seeming paper thin somehow, though the stone was identical to that of her father—our father—who had died at the age of forty-six of grief, guilt, and the grinding arrears of his sorrow. I was buffeted by the wind as I hugged myself and stared. Looking into the gray gravestone against the gray sky, I felt as if I were looking far back into the past where, long before Betsy and I were born, terrible things were done to children that could not be undone, and that legacy had been passed on to us, unseen and undeserved. And in that place of knowingness—the creative unconscious—my sister and I had communicated for a brief time. Loved deeply for a brief time. And then she was gone.

I remember that day when we stood in that graveyard in St. Charles, Illinois, beside the Fox River, I had long believed the origin of my own torture lay in the death of my baby sister. I had been replaying the story for a long time that began with the toddler lying on the couch, dying before my eyes, while my parents worked in the garden and ate lunch, doing nothing to help. Betsy had eaten cold medicine. She got into a bottle of it, probably thinking it was candy. My mother was doing laundry.

That sunny autumn day, Betsy and I had been playing in that gray, undistinguished house at the top of the staircase on the second-floor landing. After a while, Joan, our mother, came back upstairs from the basement and saw white powder on the seventeen-month-old's lips.

"What did you do?" she screamed.

Although it happened when I was just three, I still have a vivid memory of my mother's raw rage.

I remember watching as Betsy lay unconscious on the living room couch. My five-year-old brother and I were standing there staring at her. My father didn't take Betsy to the hospital, though she would have received immediate treatment there. All the staff knew Dr. Cummins. He didn't even try to treat her himself. He simply went out to the garden and dug in the dirt until lunchtime. (I found out later he thought she would sleep it off.) So we ate lunch. Our family sat at the dining room table within sight of my Betsy, who lay on the couch dying.

At some point later in the evening, I remember standing in the bathroom door, watching my father hold Betsy over the bathtub and stick his finger down her throat in an effort to make her vomit. Then my parents took Betsy and left us alone. Betsy never came back home. And nobody ever told me what happened to her. She was just gone.

A turning point came the day of the funeral. Betsy was dead and buried. My last hope for an ally had vanished. I understood that those people who were supposed to be caring for me actually meant me harm. They had stood by doing nothing while Betsy died. They might let me die too. I was terrified. I needed an escape.

I remember my mother and grandmother were both at the house after the funeral. In fact, they were on the very landing where Betsy had eaten the cold medicine. I looked from woman to woman, trying to discern which one was worse. And using the small bit of logic that a child has at that age, I chose to speak to my grandmother. The child's brain naturally picks up subtle cues from the environment—sights, smells, sounds. I could not yet think that my own mother would mean me deliberate harm. I knew only that I needed to be out of the environment of that house. It was the house, the place, the setting that had killed Betsy. In a panic, I grabbed my grandmother's legs, saying, "Can I come live with you? This place is scary!"

And my grandmother just pushed me away, saying, "No."

She said it in such a demeaning, dismissive way. I think that if she had yelled, I would have felt more significant. I simply felt that I didn't matter at all—brushed away without a second thought.

I had tried connecting person-to-person. I had tried asking for what I needed—using my voice, albeit my small three-year-old voice. I had tried fight or flight. Fight wasn't possible. I was too little. So I had chosen flight by asking my grandmother to spirit me away. To take me to her house, that's all I wanted at that moment of intense terror. There was nowhere to run once my grandmother refused me. Now I had but one strategy left: I shut down. I froze. I collapsed to the floor and went into a state of deep dissociation. My breathing and heart rate slowed. I was barely alive. I couldn't hear anything, and no one could hear me. I felt unreachable. I felt so far away, and I could not reach out. In effect, I died. I have no idea how long I stayed that way. In fact, years later, my cardiologist, Craig Reiss, confirmed I had suffered from broken heart syndrome, in which extreme stress by itself can cause the heart to malfunction, in some cases for long periods of time. It can even be fatal.

I didn't say another word for a year. And it is a testimony to how damaged my family was that no one really thought to comment or act on that fact. No one took me to a doctor and said, "This child has stopped speaking. Something must be wrong." My own father could have done something, but he did not.

Everyone pretended that things were going on as normal. They certainly were anything but normal.

My memory of that time is all but blank. My mother merely fed me when mealtime came and put me to bed when nighttime came. She did not tuck me in, did not kiss me good night. She merely put me away, as you would put a doll on a shelf.

A few weeks after Betsy died, I was home alone with my mother. My brothers were at school. Joan packed me in the car and drove to a bridge over the Fox River. She parked the car and picked me up and got out. She went to the railing with me holding her hand and looked out over the rushing water and then at me. I don't know how I knew, but I was certain that Joan was about to jump—and take me with her. But some small spark must still have lived in that broken heart of hers. She must still have been able to have some dim feeling within her frozen self. My mother looked down at me, and she just couldn't do it. But I remember distinctly feeling that terror once again.

Father

I lived a life of terrors that would come unpredictably and, so far as I could tell, would never stop. I grew up terrified of my mom. Her rages were the predator. I was the prey. I had to remain constantly on guard to stay focused on her cues; that way I could anticipate and calm her rages before they got out of control. My brothers weren't nearly as good at it as I was. I became the expert.

I had originally thought that all of my troubles stemmed from Betsy's death, but as I examined my story over the years, and as I pursued my career as a therapist, I gradually came to a different interpretation. I no longer believe my parents were disturbed because Betsy died. I believe they were deeply disturbed from the start. They had arisen like spirits out of some shadowy trauma that lay deep in the past. I think Betsy died because of their problems.

We were born into a dangerous family. Both my

parents were very intelligent, and both were terribly broken. I knew that truth at a very young age, but I didn't want to know that I knew it because the terror was incredibly profound. If they let Betsy die right in front of our eyes, then I knew I was truly, utterly alone. I have gradually come to the conclusion that all of my mother's symptoms stemmed not from the death of my sister but from the catastrophic inheritance of my sorrowing family.

I also came to believe that my plight of being trapped and immobilized, with no hope of escape, caused me to have a freeze response, become mute, and caused damage to my heart and my hearing that have lasted a lifetime. It led to my lifelong battle to stake my own claim to a life and a unique identity that was free of the gripping control of that toxic family. And it eventually led me to work hard through somatic therapy, through physical training, through more traditional therapy, through meditation, and through years of research to recover myself—to rebuild my life and reclaim the soul that I believe was stolen from me in those years in St. Charles under the tragic spell of my family.

Some people may have trouble with the word "soul," which has a long and difficult history going back many hundreds of years. Donald Kalsched, a Jungian analyst dealing with trauma, details this in his book *Trauma and the Soul*. But in working with my clients who have had catastrophic early trauma, I feel they have lost an essential part of themselves, that eternal heart. So whether we use the word "soul" or some other term, we have a deep sense of self that—in the traumatized child—is lost or hidden and needs to be reanimated. This is the path to healing. For me, this has meant an experience of embodied safety. A shift from a feeling of constant dread —and a sense of pure helplessness—to a mind-body state of peace.

Learned helplessness occurs when a person feels completely incapable of avoiding painful situations—the sense of hopelessness someone experiences when they believe they have no control over the events in their life and absolutely no ability to alter the situations. Martin Seligman first observed "learned helplessness" in his study with dogs in the 1960s. Dogs exposed to repeated shocks they could not control did not try to escape on their own to prevent the shocks. Experimenters physically had to pick up the dogs and move their legs at least twice before the dogs attempted to escape on their own.

In my clinical experience many traumatized people suffer the same sense of immobility. They sense their body has been stuck in fight, flight, or freeze for most of their lives. Doing recentering with clients—an exercise I share at the end of the book—is a form of "moving our legs," as it were. It gives a sense of efficacy and the option to have a different sense of ourselves and of a reality where new possibilities can occur. For many, it feels like freedom and gaining a sense of personal value. Moving into a positive state in the body allows people to feel free of the entrapment of trauma to experience having a choice, creating mental clarity and empowerment.

My mother had portraits made of me and Betsy and my brothers. When I was about four or five, I would catch Joan looking at the portrait of Betsy, and I would feel all this affect coming from her to Betsy. I would feel her emotion.

Somewhere deep within her there still existed a spark of life and feeling. I so desperately craved that affection for myself. Yet my mother gave none of that to my brothers and me. Only to Betsy, who was already dead. Her affect toward me felt indifferent, if not hostile. I used to think she hated me. Now I've come to think that she hated herself, perhaps in part for being incapable of loving her own children.

My father, the town doctor, was already a ruined man. He'd had a brother who was deaf in one ear. At age nine my father was told to watch his little brother. That brother ran into the street, was hit by a car, and lost the hearing in his other ear. My dad told me he became a doctor to make up for that. And yet he was unable to save his own daughter.

My trauma was compounded at every turn. As I have learned over the years of treating trauma, that is usually the case in such families. After Betsy's death, my dad fell into an abyss. Sometimes he would put his head on my shoulder, and I'd think, *Oh my God, he's drowning. I've got to keep him afloat* . . . when I was treading water myself.

Yet something in me was strong, and I continued to

try to save myself. From the age of three, I kept trying to get out of the house. When people ask me how I made it, I say I was a brat. Really. I was quietly oppositional—almost in a competition with my mother—for her not to break me. Some may call it courage or fortitude. For me, it simply felt like a fight for pure survival. By the time I was in junior high, I began thinking, *I can break out of this now*. I thought, *I'm going to be wild*. I began smoking cigarettes. There was a park a block away from my house where I hung out with the cool kids. (Or at least they thought they were cool, and I did too.)

I dreamed of adventures. I wanted to be a French translator for the United Nations. High adventure meant getting as far away from St. Charles as I could get. But my family never went anywhere. The truth is both of my parents were severely clinically depressed. My dream was to physically get away from the despair and cruelty of my parents' home. I didn't think it was really mine. It was theirs, but I didn't understand how much of that despair I carried inside of me. I always felt like I was going to live just to spite my mom. What ultimately saved me was not getting away physically but learning to trust that the Life Force/God/Universal Consciousness, whatever you choose to call it, actually did love me, and when I took a positive action for myself, I could sense its support moving me forward. I began to learn to rely on that. And that was what redeemed me.

Mine is a story of redemption because I am amazed every day that I'm here at all. I shouldn't be where I am.

I find it hard to believe that I am a successful therapist in St. Louis and came from a place where life was so devoid of joy. It hurt to live. It literally hurt to breathe. And now I cherish every day.

But it was a long road to get here. When I was a child trying to get away, my dad began to get sick. He had his first surgery for brain cancer when I was ten. He had perhaps five years to live, but no one told me that. Like everything in our family, my father's illness was shrouded in silence and mystery.

One night I found him in the bathroom. I heard his head hit the floor as he suffered a seizure. Another time I found him in the backyard having a seizure. I scared myself straight. I pulled in my horns and quit smoking. I became super-quiet and super-good and concentrated on totally mirroring my mom. That's what she craved. She had no real emotion of her own, so I had to mirror her emotion to prop her up, or else she would fly into a rage. When I was fourteen, my father was on his last legs, having his second brain surgery at the Mayo Clinic.

The last words my dad spoke to me before his surgery were, "They're opening up my head to find out how I had such a beautiful daughter." Quite a different message from my mom's. After that surgery, he was mute until he died.

At first Joan went with him to the Mayo Clinic for his treatments. She hired a maid to stay with us. But the maid was deaf, so my older brother, who was seventeen by then, would throw these incredibly wild parties downstairs while the maid was asleep upstairs. Kids would be smoking hash and weed and drinking. The rich kids from neighboring Wayne, Illinois, would come to our home and trash it. I'd cower in the kitchen trying to keep the kids from eating all the food. I had to go to school the next morning, and I needed to take a lunch. One of my brother's friends came up to the kitchen, grabbed me by the scruff of my neck, and dragged me into a coat closet. I was practically naked, wearing only pajamas. The boy attempted to rape me, and I tried to fight him off. But I was small and thin, just as I am now. My brother came charging up the stairs, totally drunk—I don't even know if he had any clothes on—and he punched the guy out and saved me from yet another trauma.

Whenever one of these parties broke up in the early morning, I would clean up. I didn't want my mom to know there'd been a party. There's that silence again, the shrouding. All of us in that house, hiding from one another, burying secret after secret. At that time, not even I could stop myself from playing that role. Instead of letting her see what her own kids were doing, I buried it all.

I was a sophomore in high school by that time. My father was undergoing his second neurosurgery. He had a scar that went from one ear to the other, and he was paralyzed on his right side. Joan needed a break from attending to him and sent me to the Mayo Clinic to take her place. I don't know what was in my mother's mind that would allow her to do that to me. Probably, once again, it was her own frozen self. She couldn't feel, so she had no awareness, no empathy.

So for that week, I walked to my dad's room through the underground mazes of the Mayo Clinic by myself. I spent each day reading to him. He had heard the song "You'll Never Walk Alone" at church. The song was written for a Rodgers and Hammerstein musical, *Carousel*, but the choir at his church had sung it as a religious song. He told me, before becoming mute, that it had special meaning for him, so I sang it to him each evening.

That week was scary and sad for the teenage girl I had become, but it was the time when I felt closest to my dad. I protected him, speaking up when the neurosurgeons came into his room when he was asleep and turned on the glaring lights. It hit me that it was like watching Betsy die. Later it occurred to me that I had done for him what I wished someone had done for me when I couldn't talk. Just to stay with me, sing to me, nurture me.

My dad's sister flew to Minnesota but stayed in her hotel room all day and never came out. When I would return to the room late at night, Louise would exclaim, "Oh my God, I thought you'd been raped!" And I asked myself, *Why wouldn't she just walk with me if she was so worried? Why wouldn't she help carry some of the emotional burden and sorrow?* There was no answer, yet she was the only one who told me the truth. A few months later she admitted that my dad would die soon.

I both loved and hated my father. Before I started

high school, he had been in the habit of hitting me with a board used to unclog the laundry chute. Yet I could never tell what infraction would bring on the abuse. Once, I was jumping on a bed, and he hit me. If I forgot to practice piano, he would hit me with the board.

When I was thirteen and in eighth grade, I had a crush on a boy. I lost track of time at a school dance and stayed out late, swimming in the emotion of the new puppy love experience like a normal teenager. My father showed up at the dance and made a scene of dragging me home. He brought out the board to hit me. He hauled me up to my bedroom and sat on the bed, waiting for me to come to him, to place myself in supplication across his lap and expose my flesh to his deranged fury. I fell to my knees, begging, "Dad, please don't do this, please don't do this. I was just ten minutes late. I won't do it again. I'm so sorry."

His response was pathetic. It was just cruel. It was so random. The fact that I had no idea how to predict the dangers in my environment made them that much more terrifying. I was always on alert, ever vigilant to the next bad thing that would come my way. And what I remember most was the feeling of humiliation. As with my grandmother, the feeling of degradation drove me into the ground.

Somehow in that confrontation with my father, I managed to get through to him, to turn my own humiliation on him like a fire and burn him with it. He sort of listened to me. Then he said, "Okay." He never hit me again, but the pain of many humiliations was still there as I watched him dying in his hospital bed.

Humiliation is one of the most damaging forms of trauma, for it signals being cast out of the group. And for social creatures such as humans, that can be a death sentence. Peter Levine, PhD, a renowned psychologist who deals with trauma, wrote that "the psychophysical patterns of trauma and shame are similar, there is an *intrinsic* association of shame and trauma. This includes the collapse of shoulders, slowing of heart rate, aversion of eyes, nausea, etc." In other words, shame, like fear, is not "just in your head." It's physical. And its physical effects can sometimes be lifelong.

During the week I spent at the Mayo Clinic, I received word that I'd been elected Christmas Queen at my high school. I should have been overjoyed at the honor. My teenage ego should have received a huge boost. And yet I was sunk in gloom—on death watch with my father and on suicide watch with my mother. Through all the years after the scene on the bridge when I was three, I felt that Joan might kill herself at any time, and I had to be there to absorb her rage, to mirror and guard her. The monster had risen from the deep mists of time with the child already in its jaws, and the child had no notion where, why, or how it all began. I was that child.

When I arrived at the airport in Chicago on my way home from the Mayo Clinic, I happened to see my mother walking toward me through the crowd. Joan was heading back to Mayo to take my place. "Mom!" I yelled.

But Joan wouldn't even look. She stormed on, staring straight ahead.

It was the closest I ever felt to that shock I felt at the age of three with my grandmother's swift rejection. I felt as if I'd been hit by a truck. It was all I could do to stay on my feet. It was a repeat of the day of Betsy's funeral. Such a complete denial of the self is always at the core of many childhood traumas. As Bessel van der Kolk, director of the National Complex Trauma Treatment Network, points out in *The Body Keeps the Score*, "traumatized children 'lose their tongues' and refuse to speak." More than a refusal, it is an inability. They long to speak but are struck mute by the violence done to them.

Mother

Today I am happily married. I am a proud grandmother. I have a bustling practice helping people transcend circumstances such as the ones I endured—in many cases, believe it or not, traumatic episodes much worse. And people learn to pull out of it, step by small step, until they are once again out in the light as I am, living life. The trauma doesn't go away. Our lives are not perfect. But the trauma takes a back seat to a life well lived. Things that were tasteless before become delicious once more. Days are full and good. People are kind and caring and communicating. Out of my silence, I learned to speak up.

Not everything is rosy all the time. Some things are bittersweet. For example, I get constant feedback from my clients about my attunement and empathy. But I'm just doing what I did as a child for my mother. I have so many clients because I'm a good mirror. It has made me a living, but there is some sadness in it for me. To be invisible, not there, was my most mastered and valuable childhood survival strategy. My job was to have no self. This is a very common occurrence for the child of a narcissistic mother.

My mother didn't hug me. She never said, "I love you." When I was in eighth grade and had my appendix removed, she refused to visit me in the hospital. She never tucked me in at night. She never gave me physical or emotional comfort. She did not make me feel safe. In fact, she told me she wanted me to be afraid of her. She never came to important school events. She liked to sew and cook but refused to teach me because she said it would be too much trouble. She taught me nothing that would have prepared me to be a mother and wife. I didn't even know how to bandage a cut.

When I was twelve, I had plantar warts removed from the soles of my feet. I had to walk home because she wouldn't pick me up in the car. When I entered her bedroom, she wouldn't let me sit on her bed to talk to her. She said it would wear out the mattress. She never visited me when I was in college at Duke University. Once, my flight home from North Carolina was late. She wouldn't wait at the airport. Instead she let me figure out how to get home on my own. The idea of snuggling with her child was repulsive to her. Once, we went on a trip, and I had to sleep with her. Every time I moved, she punched me in the back. We never had fun together. Her anger and lack of protection were what I sought to escape. And I did, through many years of psychological and spiritual work.

Mother

When I was in kindergarten, I would walk home at midday to have lunch. One day Joan served me corned beef hash. Abused and neglected children often have digestive troubles and find it difficult, if not impossible, to eat certain foods. I couldn't eat the hash. Just looking at it and smelling it, I could feel myself gag as my body prepared to throw up.

"You're going to sit there until you eat that," my mother said and walked away.

I sat at the table for six hours until dinner was served. I didn't say a word. She was so cold about it. Even now, as I try to describe here what I went through sitting there for all those hours, I still break down and weep. Even with as much progress as I've made in my life, I can still feel the same frozen, stuck feeling of being trapped. And I can still return to that place where I'd gone mute. Yet even at that tender age in kindergarten, I felt a fierceness rise within me. A feeling in the back of my mind set in: *I'm going to win. I'm not going to let you beat me.* I felt like I had an unbreakable steel rod inside me, making me feel invincible.

After the struggle, Joan said to that fierce little girl before her, "Well, I've broken your brothers' will, but I can't break yours." I remember her looking right at me. Inside I thought, *I am never going to let you win.* And it may have been that fierceness that ultimately saved my life.

I had a boyfriend in college from a loving Italian family. Everybody was saying, "I love you," all the time, and there was always food, good food. I'm sure I stayed with him much longer than I should have just to get that warm, loving attention. When I broke up with him, I got kind letters from his cousins and his second cousins—oh, I longed for a family like that! My parents' house was high Episcopalian, middle class, WASP. Remarkably, through creativity there was a glimmer of human hope and warmth under my mother's cold exterior. Joan was a good painter. She did beautiful needlepoint. Although she wouldn't teach me, I admired those artistic talents in her. That was something good and perhaps the tiniest glimmer of hope. Like the day she didn't jump off the bridge with me. Something in her was still alive. Seeing her in my mind's eye now, I feel she was looking out with a barely conscious longing for what she was missing of her own humanity. But not even I could redeem her back then.

I took attention and craved more any place I could find it. I had a very kind second grade teacher, Mrs. Bastien. She lived in my neighborhood. I would stand in her yard in the hope that she might notice me. She used to tenderly adjust my shirt collar, and I drank in that affection as if it were necessary for life, which it was! I was particularly proud of my Brownie outfit. I would stand in front of her in school, rather like a dog wanting to be petted, until she would tweak my collar, and I'd bask in that affection.

Small kindnesses could not amend how deeply,

deeply alone I've felt for most of my life. Even when good things happened, I couldn't connect with that heartfelt sense of gratitude. There was always this pain in my heart that I took, of course, as something that was bad about me. Eventually I would get over that and feel truly connected with people I love, but it was hard to get over the old, implicit learning I had done since childhood—to efface myself and guard against feeling good because I knew that as soon as I allowed myself to feel good, something terrible would happen. To come out of isolation is not for the faint of heart, but it carries untold rewards once you've done it. The lyrics of the Leonard Cohen song "Hallelujah" come to mind: "And even though it all went wrong, I'll stand before the Lord of Song with nothing on my tongue but Hallelujah."

New

I will always have my quirks, but I feel like I am in healthy relationships now. I know a lot better how to speak up for myself. Once, my husband Harry and I were on a trip. I got up early in the morning to go to the bathroom, and when I came out Harry was watching television. I wanted to sleep some more. In the past, I would have simply kept my mouth shut and been a victim. I would have withdrawn. It might have spoiled the whole trip. But with my new sense of self, my new power, I was able to speak up and simply ask Harry to turn off the television so that I could sleep a little bit more. Instead of going through our day full of resentment and loneliness and anger, I was able to dispel the incident and get on with life. And Harry didn't mind at all. I gradually began to realize that not all people sulk and seethe like my mother. You can actually tell people what you want, and if they are truly your friends and family, they will delight in pleasing you. It was a completely foreign concept.

In *The Body Keeps the Score*, Bessel van der Kolk wrote, "The emotions and physical sensations that were imprinted during the trauma are experienced not as memories but as disruptive physical reactions in the present." I had learned to let my thinking brain overtake those feelings and to master them in order to redirect my behavior to new and better paths.

Another gift of the new learning was that I felt my children were on their true life's course. One of the most important elements of my healing was being able to feel gratitude for being given the chance to live. It's not as if those disruptive feelings are totally eradicated. But I don't act on them anymore. And that is one of the things I love helping people with. My dream had always been to have a happy family. When my children were little, I'd have all the neighborhood kids over to play, and I just loved that. My son Bobby made a golf course in the yard where they'd play for hours. Or I'd let the kids come in and finger paint. They could even paint the walls! I allowed them the carefree moments of childhood I never experienced.

My children are from my first husband. That's why my name is Jones, not Cummins. I think if I'd had a different kind of first husband, I would have had at least four kids instead of two. But now with my children grown and established in their own lives, I have seen my dream of a family come true.

Because of the impact the early trauma had on my heart, I never had any stamina; still I wanted to be a runner. In college, I would run around the track chanting the lines from *The Little Engine That Could*: "I think I can. I think I can. I think I can . . .!" But the only result was that I would get purple in the face, unable to complete my goal of running two miles. This was just more proof that I was not enough; my sense *there is something deficient in me* was reinforced. In 2010 after two heart surgeries, I started to train to run a mile. Then, after being inspired by watching a friend run the Chicago Marathon, I decided to aim for that! Not the entire twenty-six miles, but six of them. It was a dream come true. Bobby joined me. He ran a half-marathon, and we met up six miles away from the finish line. I am overjoyed by the memory of participating and crossing the finish line, but it was a process.

I showed up to a gym for the first time in my life when I was barely able to walk after having heart surgery. With the help of my amazing trainer, Mike Jaudes, I wound up running a five-kilometer race a year later. A dear friend had recommended I get professional help, and I did. Mike owns The Fitness Edge in St. Louis, where I began training under his encouragement and expertise. One time, as we worked together, he mentioned my rotator cuff, and I thought, *Rotator cuff? I have a rotator cuff?* My view of myself was so damaged and defective that I felt as if I might be an alien. Mike began to give me back my body. Trauma is about the body, and once the body is compromised, it's difficult for a survivor to feel safe, even in her own body. We have to find a way to regain that connection with our body, and that is precisely what Mike began to teach me.

He'd say, "Do twenty push-ups."

And I'd say, "I can't do that!" But then I would go ahead and do it and astonish myself. Then the next time, I'd say the same thing again. But after four or five times, my brain began to catch on that I was actually doing it. And my body began to celebrate its own successes by making me feel better. It was slow. It was deep. It was personal. And it worked. Running in the Chicago Marathon! These are the miracles that can come from addressing childhood trauma and taking new control of your life.

Borderline

Because of my mother's disorder, I never formed a healthy attachment with her. Joan never gave me those vocal or tactile signals that told me I could feel safe with her. That subterranean world of thought and feeling is "the unthought known." A British psychologist named Christopher Bollas coined the term. It represents the things you know that you don't realize you know.

In her book *Understanding the Borderline Mother*, Christine Ann Lawson writes that people suffering from this disorder "may sulk or become enraged when not receiving adequate mirroring. [Borderline] mothers are unable to provide adequate mirroring for their children because of their own need for attention." Lawson lists behaviors the borderline mother does or fails to do and compares them with those traits of an adequate or even ideal mother. The ideal mother comforts her child, apologizes for inappropriate behavior, takes care of herself, encourages independence in her children, is proud of her children's accomplishments, builds her children's self-esteem, responds to her children's changing needs, calms and comforts her children, disciplines with logical and natural consequences and not out of proportion, expects that her children will be loved by others, never threatens abandonment, believes in her children's basic goodness, and trusts her children.

Like Joan, the borderline mother does not apologize for—or even remember—her own inappropriate behavior. She expects to be taken care of, punishes or discourages independence, envies, ignores, or demeans her children's accomplishments, destroys, denigrates, or undermines self-esteem, expects children to respond to her needs, frightens and upsets her children, disciplines inconsistently or punitively, feels left out, jealous, or resentful if the child is loved by someone else, uses threats of abandonment (or actual abandonment) to punish the child, does not believe in her children's basic goodness, and does not trust her children.

At the very moment when I needed safety signals from my mother, I was given signals that a predator was near. That predator was none other than my own mother. This kind of abuse makes it difficult to tell who's a predator and who is not later in life. In fact, I married an abusive man and knew it was a mistake the very day of my wedding. I embraced a predator right in my own home because I had never learned what it felt like to be safe.

Although from the age of three I attempted to look normal, I was a deeply sad and lonely child. When I was about seven or eight years old, my mother used to take me to a barbershop to get my hair cut. Although I wanted long hair like my cousin, my mother would insist on me getting a pixie cut. I hated how boyish pixie cuts looked.

The barber cut my hair as instructed. Since Christmas was just a few days away, he sprinkled some green glitter on top of my head. Then he said something to me that has stuck with me my entire life: "Always remember: you sparkle!"

This unknown person was so empathetically attuned to me, he could see beneath my attempt to be okay—to be "normal." He could sense my suffering and offered this intensely compassionate and kind act of glitter and loving words. I sparkle. In the decades that followed, in the really dark times I could hear his voice and words of comfort and confidence. In my thirties I tried to find him to thank him—to tell him how that act of kindness had impacted me so deeply and enduringly, but the barbershop was long gone. I made sure the magic lived on as I would put green glitter in my children's hair during Christmas. I've also told many clients this story to illustrate how a simple, kind gesture may change someone's life, yet we may never know.

In the 1962 movie *The Manchurian Candidate*, Angela Lansbury plays a character named Mrs. Eleanor Shaw Iselin, who has conspired to brainwash her son and program him to kill the president of the United States. That movie is not about spies and international intrigue. It's about what a narcissistic mother with borderline personality disorder can do to her child.

There are four kinds of borderline personality disorders. The Hermit, as the name suggests, is reclusive. She stays at home and isolates herself to create a little world that almost surely includes a dependent person to mirror her and do her bidding. The Waif is helpless. Her dependent person—that's me—has to continually save the Waif. The Queen is dominant and has to exert control over everything, especially over her dependent person. The Witch is mean. Borderline mothers can be a mixture of all four but usually have a trait or two that will dominate the personality. So I think my mom was the Witch and the Hermit. And I was the good child. I watched my mother pick up my children when they were little. She was very tender with them. I watched her pick them up as newborns, and I couldn't believe my eyes. I think she was really good with children until they were one year old; then, as soon as we children differentiated at all, that's when the Witch and Hermit took control.

I once asked my mother why she even had children if she didn't want them to have a life. Her answer was, "I didn't want to be alone." The terror of the borderline is abandonment. Therefore, it makes sense they use their children as narcissistic objects. The message I got from my mother was that I had a use, but I was of no value. I could be useful for someone or belong to someone, but I couldn't just be me; that was useless. This had the effect of making me compensate by trying to be competent in the world outside myself, rather than looking at the world within, which was the source of my pain.

My journey to freedom, as I call it, involved overcoming that original failed escape to my grandmother's house when I was three. And the second part was really understanding these self-destructive patterns with my mom, which were so deeply unconscious. We don't even know we're doing them, so we carry them into our other relationships. It's so deeply ingrained as a survival mechanism, it takes a lot to get conscious of them. And a lot more to change them.

I did carry those patterns into my next relationship. I graduated from Duke in 1975 and married a man named James Jones. Jim was a navigator in the Navy in A-6 fighter planes flying off of aircraft carriers. I was left alone for long stretches of time. While he was gone, I would visit my mother and fall back into the old pattern. I felt responsible for her and still afraid of her. When my husband was transferred to Whidbey Island in Washington State, my mother came and searched out every speck of dust in the home so she could critique my housekeeping. By that time, I was pregnant. I was going through all the same old patterns of behavior with my mother that were left over from my childhood, and yet I had no idea what I was doing. Years later, when Jim Jones was gone and I was married to Harry, my second husband, he pointed out that this is precisely when people start considering therapy, because their lives seem to be under the control of an evil spirit, and they have no idea why they're doing the self-destructive things they're doing. It all seemed perfectly normal to me, except now I could literally feel that it was wrong. I was completely disconnected from my own inner voice . . . my own soul.

I've been searching my whole life for what was wrong with me. My body hurt. It felt like I'd put my hand in an electric socket. It was painful not just to be in my life but to be in my body. Loving and nurturing brings physical comfort. Withholding that comfort causes profound pain. Yet I sabotaged myself time and time again.

For example, my dream as a teenager was to go to Hawaii. I've always loved the beach and even wanted to go to college in Hawaii. Since my mother wouldn't pay for my travel to and from college, I couldn't go there. But when James Jones was posted there by the Navy, I had a chance to visit him. I was ecstatic. And this is the cruelest thing about these disorders that are brought on by childhood trauma. I had the chance to make a clean getaway. I could have put thousands of miles between me and my mother. What did I do? I invited my mother to come along! I know. It makes sense only if you understand the iron grip that the borderline mother has on her child.

As the departure date grew closer, my mother became more and more negative. She started complaining about the arrangements, the finances. She became hostile. I remember one conversation on the phone when she was criticizing me for something having to do with the trip, and I went mute with her. I shut down.

Your body knows when you're doing something wrong. Your own body can often rise up and try to warn you about the wrong path you're on. The body never lies. A few days after that confrontation with my mother, I noticed that my ring finger was hot. It had a tiny cut. I hadn't given it much thought. And of course, I was not even aware of the astounding poignancy of the moment: I was trapped between an abusive mother and an abusive husband, and my ring finger got infected! I went to the doctor, and he gave me some antibiotics. A few days later I noticed a red line moving from my hand up my arm. I went to the emergency room, and the doctor put me on IV antibiotics. I had sepsis. The doctors even debated whether they should amputate my hand to save my life.

The legacy of childhood trauma can be lethal.

Now here I was, it was the middle of a dreary February in St. Louis, and I was supposed to be on the beach in Hawaii. I never got there. It was only later that I realized I had unconsciously made myself sick so I didn't have to confront my mom. Or my husband. It was less painful for me to endure all that physical agony than to see how little I meant to my own mother. I would rather have lost my hand than deal with the psychic pain of not really existing in Joan Marguerite Sill's mind and heart. I was also terrified to see my husband and to have to face the fact of what a mistake it had been to marry him.

Unconscious

I always believed that Betsy's death was my fault. After my collapse, I frequently fainted. Sometimes I banged my head on hard things such as the metal base for the clothesline in the backyard. My father, the doctor, said I would grow out of that behavior.

Yet my body, my unconscious, was desperately trying to get the message through to me. It did astonishing things to try to alert me. In fourth grade I dressed up like a broken heart for Halloween. I did not yet consciously know that all the trauma had physically damaged my heart so badly that I would one day require open heart surgery. But my body knew. I knew it through what Stephen Porges calls "neuroception," and my body made me paint a broken heart on poster board and wear red tights and a red turtleneck and stand up all day in school to scream out my silent and desperate cry for help.

Neuroception, a term coined by the behavioral

neuroscientist Stephen Porges, PhD, refers to unconscious perceptions that we constantly pick up but that do not rise to the level of consciousness. "Neuroception is not perception," he says. "Neuroception, distinct from perception, does not require an awareness of things going on. We have to throw away the word 'perception.' It is detection without awareness." Michael Gazzaniga, PhD, director of the SAGE Center for the Study of the Mind at University of California, Santa Barbara, uses the term "nonconscious processing." Whatever term we use, these messages manifest themselves as physical feelings and as actions. Porges would eventually interview me and conclude that I had, indeed, experienced damage to hearing, heart, and vagal nerve through childhood trauma.

At age seven or eight, I would leave home and go to the park and swing endlessly, soothing myself into flight in a monotonous trance. The physical patterned rhythms, the forces of acceleration against and within my body, gave me comfort in a world where there was none. It was freedom safely embodied. And the agency of willing myself into motion made me feel as if I had some control in a world that was clearly out of control. As a result of all that practice, I was a great swinger. I could swing higher than anybody. I could swing so high that I could actually touch my toes to the leaves of the trees. Years later as an adult, when I began to go to therapy, I used that as an example of a time when I felt most capable and efficacious. Doing something positive for yourself is always part of the process of healing.

My childhood memory is nearly blank until I went to kindergarten. I really, really liked school. I was good at school, and I was well liked at school. The teachers liked me, and surprisingly, given my mental state, I had a lot of friends. I really believed something was wrong with me, but in fact, I was functioning extremely well. I also liked school because it gave me a sense of efficacy. I liked to learn, and I liked reading books a lot. Staying busy eased my anxiety. As soon as I was old enough, I began working. At fifteen I worked two jobs just to stay away from the house.

I was the first girl in kindergarten to have a boyfriend. I'm not sure how much I really enjoyed the boys at school and their attention. I may have unconsciously used it as a way to counter my mother's message that Betsy was the pretty one. I was using it as a defense, more than enjoying it in a healthy way.

My girlfriends and teachers liked me and served much the same purpose. I never let on to any of them what I was going through at home. It wasn't until college that I told my best friend, Robin Ferracone, what had happened to me: the molestation, the abuse, and Betsy's death. But they were just words, and they came out flat, as if I'd told her that I preferred Coke over Pepsi. I could say it as a fact, but I still could not feel how it had influenced my life. Indeed, what I reported to my friend was not the essence of what was eating at me.

My collapse and near-death experience after Betsy's death actually saved my sense of having any worth at all. When I was in that limbo—mute, alone, frozen, disassociated from my body and from the world—I continued to feel that sense of goodness. In that state, I felt this very, very loving, enveloping Presence. It was so comforting. I call it my guardian angel. It's not like I saw a being with wings or anything like that. The child needs something to hold on to, to feel that somebody cares. And this Presence was and still is my guardian angel. Many children who have had near-death experiences talk about this as a light that they either see or feel. You trust with your whole heart that you are in divine loving care.

Kalsched wrote in *Trauma and the Soul*, "Survivors of early trauma often report an essential part of themselves has retreated into a spiritual world and found refuge and support there in the absence of that support by any person." In fact, as a very young child, I remember having Santa Claus as my representation of the Life Force and love—someone caring about my well-being. Little children will take comfort wherever they can find it. Later on, I transferred that concept to Jesus. By the time I was ten years old, I'd walk to church five miles each way on Good Friday just to sit with Jesus. It really doesn't matter how we choose to represent this Presence, this unconditional love, but to believe in it will help us survive. Kalsched calls this the "achievement of a higher innocence." He refers to this process as the "Lifegiver." The term was coined by the psychoanalyst Neville Symington, who was known for his studies of narcissism. The older, lost innocence is really always there, but like the sun, it may be obscured by clouds.

During my year of being mute, sustained by that Presence, I felt as if I were given the choice of whether I would come back to the world or not. I could have gone over and died like Betsy. I felt I was experiencing the Life Force, although I didn't yet know that phrase. It was very loving; all of it was sweetly loving. I could feel my guardian angel loving me, and that was a great comfort. Part of me wanted to be on the other side because my sister was there. But it was a double bind. I felt that if I went to the other side, I would have love but no life. But if I stayed in my life, there would be no love. Of course, as a child, I couldn't articulate all of that. It was all negotiated within me by way of neuroception and feelings. But even so, from the vantage of adulthood, it was not an easy choice. I felt as if my guardian angel gave me a choice. And I decided to come back. However, I came back into this body that was so malfunctioning that I felt like I was in a space suit that had been fried. And yet I felt like I'd brought back a piece of heaven with me. There was a good part of that experience as well because I knew what it was like to feel that kind of love, centered in safety and belonging. That was what enabled me to not let my mom break me and to get to the place where I am today. And I want to give encouragement to other people that that kind of love is real. We all have a guardian angel we can reach out to when we really need to either in the spiritual realm as I experienced or in the physical world—those who love and support us unconditionally.

Part of my real struggle in choosing between life and

death was that I did not want to say good-bye to Betsy. She was my light. She was the little light that was in that house. I feel as though my guardian angel took me to visit her one last time when I collapsed and went mute.

I had to choose between life and death another time in my life too. After open heart surgery I was then faced with having to undergo another similar operation some years later. For a week or so I was really thinking, *I'm not going to do it*. I wasn't suicidal, and I was not adopting the role of a victim. I just really, really didn't think I could do it again, but once I realized my job was to do the next right thing, I also realized that I wanted to try to convince other people to make similar choices and do something constructive and positive when they are in the worst possible position. I think of Viktor Frankl describing prisoners in a Nazi death camp stopping to appreciate the beauty of a sunset, even though they knew they might never experience freedom again.

I decided I wanted to be a voice for the fact that there is something good in the world, that there is beauty and love and light. In addition, it was the ultimate defiance of my family that was in such despair. I wanted to say, "No, something different can come from that pain. There's something much better than giving in to that despair and giving up. There *is* more to life."

As I grew from child to adolescent to teen to adult, more and more times people would remark that there was something different about me. I call it "touched by an angel." I tried to hide those experiences for a long time from my family almost as a way to preserve them. I was afraid they'd try to wreck it for me, but now I want to share them so that others can have the same experience. As the subtitle of Stephen M. Johnson, PhD's *Characterological Transformation* suggests, to move from a sense of isolation to a sense of connection is, in many ways, a "hard-work miracle" that starts with believing a different mindset and experience of safely being embodied is possible.

Danger

My first child was due April 27, 1977. Joan flew out for the birth. When the baby wasn't born on her due date, Joan was furious with me that she had to wait. Sarah was born on May 2 to a stressed and terrified mother. As Robert Sapolsky, PhD, an expert on stress at Stanford University and recipient of a MacArthur Fellowship, has pointed out, an elevated level of stress hormones in the mother teaches the fetus that danger is near.

Fetuses can monitor signals of stress from the mother, insofar as glucocorticoids (stress hormones) readily pass through to the fetal circulation, and ample glucocorticoids "teach" the fetus it is indeed a stressful world out there. The result? Be prepared for that stressful world: Tend toward secreting excessive amounts of glucocorticoids, which can increase the odds of obesity, insulin-resistant diabetes, and hypertension.

Indeed, communication between mother and fetus

by way of stress hormones is a chemical code—a warning that requires no conscious awareness—telling the baby to be prepared because things are going to get bad. In this case, being prepared means a life of constant alertness, tension, and high stress hormones. That in turn can lead to all sorts of health problems. In 1995 the Centers for Disease Control and Prevention began a study to understand the effects of abuse and neglect in childhood. Called the CDC-Kaiser Adverse Childhood Experiences (ACE) Study, it collected data from seventeen thousand people that related childhood experiences to health later in life. It clearly showed that disruption of normal development in early childhood led to the symptoms I've seen in my own life and in the people I see in my therapy practice. Abuse and neglect also leads directly to disease and to behaviors that can cause an unhappy life and an early death. The CDC provides an abundance of information on the subject, including questionnaires that anyone can take to measure risk. (Search "adverse childhood experiences.") The CDC estimates that one in four people has suffered abuse or neglect in childhood, yet it is surprisingly difficult for someone to recognize the symptoms in themself, as my own story shows.

There is another aspect—a warning that Levine and others give to their clients. If you have been traumatized and abused, predators can sense it through neuroception. They target you because they know, even if only unconsciously, that you are more likely to freeze, more likely to forget, and more likely to keep silent afterward.

So being traumatized puts you at greater risk of being traumatized again.

Nearly all my colleagues in trauma therapy say they commonly see people coming to them in midlife for these complaints because they have been coping with their disabilities and masking their symptoms—from others and from themselves—until the dam bursts and their lives can no longer hold together.

As it was with me. And when I was pregnant, in a bad marriage, and assaulted by my mother, I began reading compulsively, unconsciously trying to educate myself so I could figure out why I was behaving the way I was and could then plan an escape. Through this unconscious neuroception, I recognized that I was defenseless and at the mercy of those two dangerous people: my mother and my husband. I equated education with competence.

Long before I became consciously aware that there was anything wrong with my marriage, my body was forcing this behavior on me. The answers are always all around us if we allow them in. For me, one big hint about the tremendous mistake I had made came even before I arrived home from my wedding. I married James Jones in 1975 in St. Charles, Illinois. And as we got into the limousine to go to the reception, this wave of doom came over me that I had not felt before at all in relation to Jim. After all, we had just gotten married.

We were supposed to be glowing with joy. But inside the limousine, when I turned to look at him, he wouldn't look at me. When Jim and I were in the line at the reception, smiling, shaking hands, giving air kisses, he finally turned and looked at me. Jim leaned over and growled into my ear, "Your ass is mine." I was in complete shock. He had never spoken to me that way before. For just as neuroception can be screaming out at us beneath the surface, the abused child—who has learned not to hear and learned not to see—can be remarkably adept at turning a deaf ear to the most obvious messages of danger.

He had been a perfect gentleman before the marriage. He was attentive and kind, giving me what I had craved all my life but had never had. I was a sitting duck for his intentions toward me during our courtship. I was completely defenseless. Then, after the wedding—on the very day of the wedding—all that changed. It was like a switch flipped on. Getting married to me was like a thing on his list that he crossed off, and I was an unwitting target. Jim had joined the Navy and was put in flight training at Pensacola. When we moved to Florida, he was a completely different man. He became absorbed in his naval program and shut down.

Around 1980, when I was in my thirties, I began to study dysfunctional families. At the time I thought our problems stemmed from Jim's being in the Navy and having to spend so much time away from the family. You know those cruises, you're gone for six or seven months at a time. I kept wanting to have a normal family. I thought that if Jim were around like a regular husband, that would fix everything. But gradually my mind began to change; it began to occur to me that maybe there was something dysfunctional about our family. As I began telling Jim my thoughts and began suggesting that we might need therapy, that we might need change, he began to get violent. The more I pleaded for help—for the sake of the children—the more violent he became.

My body spoke to me again when I began to test positive for the precursors of cervical cancer. I lay in the bathtub contemplating my future and realizing I had to make some changes or my life would be in danger—as would the well-being of my children. I struggled with myself because on the surface I had everything a woman could wish for: a smart, handsome husband, two cute kids, and a nice house. The facade was like the gray house of my childhood in St. Charles, looking so normal on the outside. Underneath it all was my sickening realization that I simply didn't like my narcissistic husband and his violent ways. Yet it was not clear to me what I could do. Then one night Jim got so angry that he pushed me through a wall. He actually broke the wall, that's how hard he pushed me. Both of the children saw him do it. This is exactly the point I was making earlier when I said that people come to therapy in midlife asking, "Why am I doing this?" In my mind I asked at last why I was putting up with this.

I tried again and again to make it work. "You grew up in a shame-based household," I pleaded with Jim. "I grew up in a shame-based household. Both our dads were blamed for their brothers' disabilities. Please come to therapy with me." Met with facing himself, Jim's violence grew even worse. During one altercation, he put his fist through the kitchen window.

I had reached a turning point. I graduated from Duke with a BA in psychology, but that wasn't enough to allow me to work. I realized I needed to go to graduate school and prepare myself for life on my own. Not only that, but I had to get my children out. Jim was not going to make any of these changes with me. I piled the kids into the Volvo station wagon and set out for my mother's house, planning to stay there until I could figure things out. In a welter of confusion, I pulled into a parking lot before getting on the highway and was hit by the sudden realization that if I went back to my mother's house, I'd never, ever get out. I'd just be perpetuating the same patterns as before.

As Bessel van der Kolk says in his book *The Body Keeps the Score*, "Scared animals return home, regardless of whether home is safe or frightening." In fact, years later I would realize how entrenched in my family I was. When you're in a family, you don't notice that sort of thing. Those people are just your family—your own reality. Moreover, after trauma we no longer make sense to ourselves. We can't tell our own story as a coherent narrative. Traumatized people try to explain themselves, but they get their tenses mixed up, their speech breaks up—as mine did for a long time—they're not able to find the words easily. My story of what was going on in my life eluded me because I was incoherent in trying to explain it to myself, but it gradually began to dawn on me what was going on.

After Pensacola, Jim moved the family to a suburb of Chicago called Wilmette. I loved the house, the neighborhood, the schools for the kids. But now I was near enough to my mother and grandmother that I felt I might never escape the family. I was not yet schooled in psychology well enough to realize how much danger I was in. I was a slave to what I call The Thirteenth Commandment: Thou shalt not displease thy mother. And the worst part was that I wasn't even aware of the predicament I was in. I wasn't even trying to leave my mother and grandmother. I was just trying to dismantle the pattern of behavior and pain. And I instinctively knew that I couldn't count on support from anyone. It's just like any addict who wants to get better does not necessarily get support from the system he came from. Actually, the opposite is true.

At the same time, I realized I could have stayed where I was if I'd been willing to put up with the physical and emotional abuse, with the bullying from my mother and grandmother, the disrespect and condescension. If I'd been willing to sacrifice my children, I could have stayed and lived out my life the way many people do in quiet misery. I would never have had to work. But it was that stubborn streak in me and that boundless curiosity that kept me going. And it was the pure love for my children. I started my career because I had to become economically viable. In 1987 I went to graduate school. I ran away to Duke and was accepted to the graduate psychology program. But my mother kept sucking me back in. I wanted to break away from my mother with finality. I needed my own life, but I was brainwashed. I had no clue how programmed I was. Nevertheless, the timeline from the early eighties when Jim pushed me through the wall until I finished my master's degree and took an internship at a children's hospital spanned about seven years. I like to compare myself to Tim Robbins in the movie *The Shawshank Redemption*, based on a novel by Stephen King. Robbins played Andy Dufresne, who was wrongly imprisoned and fought little by little for years to get out.

My daughter Sarah confronted her father about the incident when he pushed me through a wall, and he denied that it ever happened. "Your mother just makes things up," he said.

Sarah protested. "Dad, number one, I saw you do it, and number two, the hole is still there. It's right in the hallway. I see it every time I walk down the hall."

In many ways, I was recreating with Jim the experience I'd had with my own father. He was always, always working. So I unconsciously chose a man to be my husband who would remove himself from the family. In one case, he took a job that would keep him away at a secret location for an entire year. I managed to discover that he was in Fort Worth, Texas, and I visited him there. I had begun to see the patterns and realize that my dream of having a normal family would never come true in my present situation. And yet I acknowledge how very painful it is just to really look at the family dynamics and try to become more conscious of it and also make the changes within yourself that are necessary to make. It's hard, and it's painful.

My body was screaming at me, trying to get my attention. During my first year of marriage, I began thinking that I ought to get divorced. What I did instead, which is very interesting, was to go to work at a Montessori school, and I kept getting strep throat so bad that I couldn't talk. Only later, upon reflection, did I see that my body was replaying my experience of going mute as a young child. I wound up having to quit my job. And although the thoughts of leaving Jim continued, I still felt trapped. I had no family support—certainly not from my mother—and I had no internal resources either. I had virtually no self-awareness. I remember thinking, *I've got to leave him*, but I didn't have the strength.

Heart

I realized later in life that I had been brought up not to engage socially. If I ever had a question as a child, I did not ask my parents. I went to books to find the answers. In my marriage to Jim, I began to learn about attachment theory from books. I was used to looking things up, so I began to understand things like the internal working models we carry around with us that explain, often unconsciously, who we are and how relationships work and what we can expect from the world. It's the view by which you comprehend what happens to you.

Those unconscious beliefs are so incredibly powerful that they shape who you are and drive your life. And you don't even know it. That is why I loved the concept of the unthought known. I think this is a very poetic way of putting it—these beliefs that you believe but you don't even think them. They're not verbal; they're implicit. I think that's what happened to me before I even had much language. Little kids have it. We say they act on instinct, but they really know a lot. And at that age, with that wisdom of the child, I felt I was utterly alone in a completely overwhelming situation.

So in that time of trying to get away from Jim, in addition to attachment theory, I began to employ reconsolidation, which is the idea that even with an underlying set of beliefs, new learning can take place. And in the wake of that learning, the old models would eventually become obsolete. It's like we once thought the Earth was flat. We can remember that we had that thought, but we don't believe it anymore. We've seen the Earth, and it is round. While admitting that the old beliefs could be triggered by events in the environment —I could still get freaked out—my new experience was that it didn't crush me in the same way.

As an example, when I was in my sixties and a successful therapist, I was leading a group therapy session that I really loved. I always felt very open and safe in that environment. One day the group session ran over time, and I asked one of the members, who was supposed to present a piece of artwork, if she could postpone the presentation to the next week so we'd have time to do her justice and not be rushed. I went up to her at the end of the group, and she directed her full-on rage at me. She started to say incoherent things, and a part of my brain knew she was being borderline psychotic, yet the damage had been done. The direct hit of pure unadulterated vitriol had pierced my heart. I immediately felt chest pain and did so for about three hours. I kept thinking I was having a heart attack. I thought I might die from that triggering of my old flat-Earth self.

I tried to let it pass, but the next day, by chance, I had an appointment with my doctor. He listened to my heart and said I must have an EKG right away. The results were abnormal, and he said the EKG indicated a heart attack. In the emergency room, they measured enzymes in my blood and confirmed that I'd indeed had a heart attack. But when my cardiologist, Craig Reiss, came to see me, he said I had broken heart syndrome, which is different from a heart attack. Reiss is one of the leading experts on this condition, which is brought on by powerful emotions and can be fatal, as I mentioned earlier. I went in with an ejection fraction of 29 percent, which means that my heart was not pumping enough blood. It was a life-threatening condition. I was in the hospital for nearly a week, during which doctor after doctor, nurse after nurse validated my experience of being attacked by that woman. It was extremely nurturing. I am convinced this experience was a recapitulation of my early trauma. The rage being directed at me was too much for my heart to handle. But I had come to a new set of beliefs that helped me deal with it and climb back out of the dark place into which I had been catapulted by the confrontation. I had new tools. I had new skills. I had new beliefs. And I used them. Instead of receiving invalidation and rejection, I experienced consistent care and respect at the hospital, validating my broken heart. It was an actual reliving of the original event, not unlike a dark night of the soul—a deconstructing of familiar thoughts, feelings, and behavior patterns to upgrade old survival strategies. While in the hospital, I observed my inner process as my physical self was being tended to.

I acknowledged the pain of shock. How utterly alienating that is. The next layer for me under the shock was an ineffable aloneness. Not loneliness, but a profound, unspeakable sense of being *alone*. Then under that was my brain's archaic interpretation of this: *I'm alone because there's something wrong with me.* These partially unthought knowns were accessible to me through this experience. They came out of the shadow and into consciousness and were healed through somatic therapy and spiritual practices.

As I was processing these layered experiences in the hospital, I realized I needed to move my mind and body out of fear and into peace. My experience with somatic work gave me the template I needed to do this. I would imagine myself being unified with Divine Mercy. I would feel Mercy and Grace flooding my body. A much higher vibration of energy than fear and pain. I would imagine letting my nervous system go on vacation where I could rest and absorb Divine Compassion. The nurses would frequently come to report to me various measurements concerning my heart and my condition, blood pressure, heart rate, clotting factor, and so on. Each time they did so, I would experience my fear reaction once again, so I would in turn do the Mercy exercises all over again to cope with it. I practiced and practiced all that weekend. I was admitted to the hospital on a Friday, and by the time Monday came around, I could be wheeled into the testing laboratory with my body in a state of flow and without fear.

It taught me how to feel loved, lovable, and loving; I still feel it now. I had known all of these things intellectually before that, but now I believe them where it really counts: emotionally. Whereas all other hospitalizations before that had felt traumatic as I was dealing with problem after problem, this one felt therapeutic and healing.

So I took that trigger, which earlier in my life could have been crippling, and turned it into an experience of growth. I'm sharing my journey because, more than anything, I want to get across that people can get their souls back and can get their lives back. And I want people to understand that this kind of unconditional love is real—a sense of having innate value, of belonging, having an ability to be effective in the world—that I felt from what I call my guardian angel. And that's the reason I came back instead of joining Betsy. That's the reason I've been able to heal.

Flow

At the time I was trying to get away from Jim, the messages that my children and I were in grave danger kept coming hard and fast from my neuroception. I was in a state of constant hypervigilance, extremely attuned to the subtlest cues. I had become so inured to Jim's physical violence, his psychological terrorism, that for a long time I could not acknowledge the naked evidence I'd known all along but could not see: *This is exactly how I grew up with my mom.* Joan provided psychological terrorism. My father did the hitting at her behest. And now I'd married a man who did both. He was resentful and angry. He was a very bitter guy, quite similar to my mom.

Deep in my subconscious I knew that I had to save myself or I would die. I began to educate myself even more deeply about family dysfunction. My mother's outrageous behavior stopped seeming so normal to me. It began to seem outrageous. The more I read, however, the more I realized how dangerous my situation was. I found out that men who are violent to women can kill them. As the pressure to change builds, they can lose control and do real damage. They sometimes kill the children too. I had to get out.

I began going to therapy by myself. If he was unwilling to cooperate, at least I could get myself psychologically stronger. The stronger I got, the more clearly I saw Jim. And the more clearly I saw Jim, the more violent he became. He would backhand me at the drop of a hat. Both the children witnessed his attacks. They were terrified. I was terrified.

After Whidbey Island, the Navy sent him to Northwestern University to study aircraft design. He got a master's degree, and we lived comfortably in a quiet suburb on the North Shore in Illinois in a house of deceptive blandness, not unlike our house in St. Charles had been. Then he got a good job offer at McDonnell Douglas in St. Louis, so we moved there. But the marriage kept going downhill.

When Jim realized I was going to divorce him, he signed his life insurance over to his girlfriend. (Of course, he wasn't faithful. That is almost always a feature of such dysfunctional relationships.) Our divorce became final in 1993. I continued with therapy, and as I loved myself, I found true love at last with a nurturing husband in Harry. We married on a Saturday in 1996 at four o'clock in the afternoon. Four weeks after Harry and I married—once again at four o'clock in the afternoon—Jim was driving on a country road and pulled his car in front of a truck.

My newly educated state now prevented me from ignoring the dangers of my situation. I clearly saw my pattern with my mother. Joan would say something to let me know how much I sucked, and then just leave the room. One day I was in Joan's living room with the children when this happened. The unspoken protocol was that I was supposed to get up, follow her, and then placate and mollify her. But I couldn't do it. It didn't come from any strength in me—I wish I could say it did—but I just felt like a beaten dog. I could feel her fury growing in the other room. She came back out at me, again with her rage. I don't even remember what she said. Talk about an unthought known. These words came out of my mouth, just like that: "It should have been me who died, not Betsy." So I obviously really had thought that all of my life. In shock before the terrible revelation, we both drew a sharp intake of breath. And then we just stood there looking at each other. We didn't know what to do in the face of the truth that stood between us like a corpse.

I told my children: "Your dad will pick you up." An hour later, Joan showed up on my front porch.

"May I come in?" she asked.

"I don't know," I said. "I don't know. If you want to be around me, you have to be nice to me. There's not a time when we're together that I don't leave feeling hurt." I told her I would cut off all contact with her if she didn't change. And Joan behaved for a couple of months and then returned to announce she had ovarian cancer.

I had always worried about Jim and worried about my mom. I knew through neuroception what I could not articulate at the time. I really was on suicide watch, keeping those two people alive by sacrificing myself. When I became enlightened as to what I'd been doing and I stopped my suicide watch, my codependent behavior, they were both dead within three years.

In the face of it all, the chaos, the pain, I felt the spiritual Presence too. The guardian angel. I don't honestly know what it was; that's just the term I prefer to use. But there really was some kind of Presence, and I wanted to survive because of that. Sometimes I call it Spirit or the Life Force. Sometimes I think of it as a hose that's either kinked or unkinked. The Presence is always there, sometimes obscured like clouds can block the sun when we're not fully in the flow. Even then there is a sense, a knowingness. Glennon Doyle, in her book *Untamed*, calls it reconnecting to "The Knowing." There is no real image to it. It's a sense that I'm not alone. There's this thing that was loving me. I don't know how else to say it, but I do know that it saved my life. The methodology to unkink the hose, reset the connections, is a daily practice. I suppose Stephen Porges would say it's another kind of message from neuroception.

Despite the pilgrimages to church in my youth, I'm

not a religious person; that's the odd thing. I once got hit on by a priest, and I stopped going to church. But I consider myself very, very spiritual. I adopted the Virgin Mary from the Catholic religion as a surrogate mother—someone I could trust—and even today, I have statues of her around the house and in the backyard. My experience is that the Life Force is this energy, this pure loving energy. Call it what you will. I like the word "angel." But if you look for it in your time of danger and suffering, if you open your heart to its pure love, it will fill you with hope and relief and a will to live. You may be wondering how to open your heart. There are myriad contemplative practices. Part of the journey is to find several that are effective—from everyday moments like gardening or appreciating a bird's song to mindfulness, prayer, and meditation.

My husband and I go to Key West every February to get a break from the winter cold. About a half mile from our hotel is an adoration chapel; I walk to it every day. This one is located at The Basilica of Saint Mary Star of the Sea. It has a life-sized image of the Divine Mercy. This is a representation of love and light flowing from Jesus's heart. On one visit I had the thought, *What if I close my eyes and imagine that same love and light flowing in my heart?* I wondered if this was sacrilegious in some way. I forged ahead in spite of this self-doubt. As I did it, my energy shifted. There was a lightness and openness to me that wasn't there when I started. It was as though the Life Force could flow through me too!

This was not a cognitive exercise; it was fully somatic and experiential. I have come to understand this was contemplative prayer—finding unity with the Life Force. Feeling its presence in the body. I am not in any organized religion, nor am I promoting a Christian perspective. I tell this story to illustrate how critical it is to find a practice that puts one's mind and body in flow. It could be gardening, listening to music, baking bread. I believe telling people how to get into this state of flow is a little like saying, "Here, use my glasses to read!" The uniquely designed prescription that works for me may make your vision blurry. Although I offer a basic outline on how to do this, it is meant to be a launching pad to find the way that works best for you—your unique method of connecting to the Life Force, to the purest of love.

I call what I did that day in the chapel "becoming," and it has been a daily practice of mine for years. It gave me a different experience of myself and life. That my body didn't always have to feel that heaviness of depression and anxiety, that it could experience a freedom and a lightness of being. It opened me to a new narrative about myself. One that became free from the self-blame and guilt I had carried for so long to a story that held the hope that I, too, belonged and that I was loveable and worthy.

I believe, along with many trauma experts—Peter Levine, Pat Ogden, Stephen Porges—that the defects in my heart were caused by my collapse on the day of Betsy's funeral when the ancient freeze response in my brain, inherited from our ancient reptilian ancestors, slowed my metabolism and heart rate to near death. The dorsal vagus nerve runs from the brain to all the vital organs below the diaphragm. It regulates how active or inactive they are and is responsible for the so-called "diving reflex" in reptiles, in which they can dive into the water and stay immobile without breathing for long periods to escape predators. We mammals have a newer vagus nerve, too, called the ventral vagus, which mediates higher functions, such as social engagement. It controls the muscles of the face and voice so we can socialize as mammals do. Reptiles don't.

Evolution is a less than perfect system and often winds up with makeshift systems that have both good and bad qualities. This is one of them. If we are threatened, we use our highest and newest strategy: social engagement. We try to talk or smile our way out of a jam. (You can see this behavior when a puppy rolls on its back when meeting an older, bigger dog.) If social engagement doesn't dispel the threat, we go down one evolutionary rung to fight or flight. If that still doesn't work, we revert to the reptilian response of the dorsal vagus nerve, and we freeze. The trouble with that response is that we are mammals and need a lot of oxygen for the heart and brain and the muscles that mediate hearing.

A growing amount of research suggests the brain is all about movement. If you don't need to move, you have no use for a brain. And the mammalian brain is especially all about movement. Mammals play. Reptiles don't. Mammals have friends. Reptiles don't. Peter Levine writes, "We are first and foremost *motor creatures. Secondarily*, we employ and engage our observing/perceiving/thinking minds." Therefore, a big component of trauma is the result of being immobilized, but most especially being immobilized against your will. We can enjoy being immobilized in someone's arms but not in someone's jaws. And indeed, shame and humiliation are forms of immobilization and are certainly about the body. Shame causes a whole suite of physiological changes equivalent to those that result from an attack by a predator. If you're a child, you'd rather be slapped than shamed. A slap is over in a second. Shame goes on and on. A slap doesn't cast you out. Shame does. And for social creatures, as mentioned before, being out of the group is a death sentence.

I froze in response to the horror I faced in my own household at age three. I experienced immobility and shame and humiliation, as well as terror. Deprived of oxygen, my heart muscles were damaged. So was my hearing. As I grew up, the damage lay dormant, but in my fifties, I began to feel fatigued and out of breath. An echocardiogram revealed the damage, which by then was severe enough to require open heart surgery. When I was wheeled into the operating room, I knew I might not emerge alive. And just beyond my head on my right side, I felt this loving energy that was so calming. It was my guardian angel. I think of God like that. It's a force, an energy. A Life Force. It was a Presence like a piece of heaven on earth. It held peace, love, grace. It was an Observing Witness, a Great Comforter. I didn't see anything, but it felt as real and present as if my five senses could detect it. It was an experience of some Greater Reality. And we truly can connect to that. I now feel that it's there all the time, trying to connect to us. It need not be religious. It need not even be merely spiritual. You can choose your own way to think about it. It can be practical, like Porges's work. He's a scientist, and he knows that something communicates with us. His term "neuroception" contains not only good feelings but cascades of vital information.

For me, trauma recovery essentially means we have the ability to make a conscious choice for ourselves, rather than our survival reaction being our automatic, knee-jerk response. Trauma keeps us in a reactive mode that entraps us endlessly in the same survival patterns; thus, we are never free.

I have worked hard to recover from my childhood trauma. I have worked especially hard not to pass it on to my children. My household as a child was a chaotic one, characterized by violence. I slowly came to realize that my primary trauma was not the shock of seeing Betsy die as I had always assumed. It was my membership in a dangerously dysfunctional family. Seeing Betsy die simply reaffirmed what I already knew through neuroception: that I belonged to parents and grandparents and brothers and aunts who might let me die too. It was a classic setup. Children know when their environment isn't safe, and they know from a very early age. The baby knows when the mother soothes, but the baby knows terribly when she does not. My mother was the more sadistic of my two parents. In hitting me, my father was Joan's tool of rage. But the effect was the same. I became the "good girl," behaving well because I was terrified. In doing so, I exerted another form of immobility on myself, to be passive and accept whatever was forced upon me. The CDC-ACE Study addresses this too. Women who have been abused and neglected as children are seven times more likely to be raped as adults. There is a kind of chronic suffering known in psychoanalysis as the "repetition compulsion." It goes on and on and never resolves itself. It's not blaming the victim, but it means that when we've been traumatized, part of us seems to unconsciously seek out situations that are going to replicate that while hoping for a different outcome. We're trying to fix it by having a different experience in the world rather than looking inside of ourselves and feeling it there. Like someone who married an alcoholic, then divorces him and marries another alcoholic. And it makes no sense because I, for example, was always really, really afraid of looking at my pain, even though my pain was already there. There wasn't anything to be afraid of because the worst was already happening to me; I was living with it every single day of my life.

Like an autoimmune disease, this self-imposed immobility pits the self against the self and simply multiplies that suffering. When I grew up and went to college, I picked the college that was farthest away: Duke University. My mother refused to take me there. I lugged a suitcase from the airport and sat on the steps of my dorm, watching the cars arrive with the other freshmen, their fathers helping to carry their luggage, their mothers hugging their pillows in plastic bags to install their beloved children comfortably in their new lodgings.

And I remember thinking, *I don't have a pillow. I'm not one of those people who deserves to have a pillow. If I deserved it, I'd have it.* I had effectively erased my own personality, my own self, to placate my raging mother.

Not having a self turns you into what the psychologist Jerome Bernstein talks about in his book *Living in the Borderland: The Evolution of Consciousness and the Challenge of Healing Trauma*. I always felt I had one foot in this world and the other in the spiritual world. And now how my life has turned out really defies the odds, given what I was before.

It is typical that the traumatized child tends to blame herself for whatever is wrong. When I was first exposed to ideas such as those of Porges, it changed my life—saved it actually. His ideas were so profound to me because they explained my brain to me rather than making it a shameful thing. Before that revelation I thought that as a kid I had failed somehow to escape. Because of the changes I saw in myself, I became keenly interested in helping people get back their ability to use that first and highest survival strategy, social engagement, so they can be part of the human race again. I realized that since I had gone to my grandmother for comfort at age three, which is really activating that social engagement part of the brain, and that failed, afterward I never again went to anyone for comfort. (The only time I could think of was once when my daughter was very ill, I went to a Catholic shrine and asked the Virgin Mary for help. Interestingly, another mother figure.) Of course, this tendency fits perfectly with my chosen career because people come to me and tell me their problems. But rarely do I go to somebody when I'm in distress, even now. I found that my grip on joyful things in my life was extremely fragile and easily disrupted.

I had always dreamed of going to Paris and finally had a chance to go. I mentioned to a friend that I was going to Paris, and the friend waxed rhapsodic about the wonders of her Paris. I got so deflated by that, I went mute again.

I've come to understand that my sister's death left such serious damage in me that I never really believed that my dreams could come true. Going to Paris was counter to that internal working model. When my friend took the conversation away from me and made it about her, the feelings of being unseen and not valued flooded me. When memories aren't fully processed, sometimes we are actually remembering traumatic events somatically. We think it's just about the present situation, but actually our bodies are reexperiencing an earlier overwhelming event.

Something vital was being taken away from me

again. I reflected more deeply on how I make my life a vessel for others while I have struggled so much to get others to be a vessel for me. As a result, I learned not to share much with other people, learned not to ask for help. As a consequence, writing this book has been extremely hard for me because I learned as a small child to be invisible.

That's how I made it through with my mom, by being invisible. And now I'm trying to bring it all out into the sunlight. I erased myself and matched her to mitigate the blows. Speaking up for myself is really hard to do. And whenever I attempt social engagement, even now, I can feel my amygdala saying, *Don't do it! Don't do it! Don't do it!* The amygdala, of course, is the alarm center of the brain that warns of danger. And I tell myself now that I'm doing this for you. I am revealing myself, my story, my pain, my anguish, and my healing so that by reading it, you may come to know yourself. This is all I've got, and I give it to you.

Body

I gradually developed methods to bring myself and my clients back to social engagement by using the body itself as a vehicle. These somatic therapies really help you regulate yourself. I began training in Sensorimotor Psychotherapy, which was originally developed by Pat Ogden, PhD, who founded the Sensorimotor Psychotherapy Institute. I also studied Peter Levine's Somatic Experiencing, which is closely related. They're very powerful modalities because they don't employ talk therapy, which uses only the neocortex. The neocortex is the thinking part of the brain that can plan things and execute actions sequentially. I think of it as the IKEA brain. You buy an end table, and it's in pieces, but if you follow the instructions, step by step, it turns into an end table. That process uses the neocortex.

My own experience of trauma was not primarily a neocortical experience. It was barely conscious. It was much more of a body experience. I felt fear. I felt panic. I felt sick. And I ultimately collapsed in a full-body shutdown.

Talking about that in a stepwise, deliberate, logical fashion was not destined to be an effective therapy. Instead, by taking myself or my clients back through the physical experience and remastering it, reinterpreting it, the trauma could be put in its place. Once I get a client into that state, the body has this amazing, wondrous way of regulating itself, allowing someone to get out of their head.

Those two somatic techniques form the basis of my work. Once I learned them, they totally reshaped how I did my job. I do that now with almost every client I have. It gives people such a sense of empowerment. You can watch the body trying to get out of its entrapment. The process is entirely organic. Your body will tell you what to do through mindfulness, which means getting out of thinking into observing and experiencing one's feelings and sensations.

I take my clients through a mindfulness exercise to make them more aware of what's going on around and within them. For severely traumatized people, that can be difficult to access. Some people never, ever, ever feel out of fight or flight. They essentially live in a state of constant panic. In that first step, I teach them how to feel safe within themselves. They can be aware of their own bodily state and recognize intellectually that they're in my office and that they are safe there. I get them to remember a time when they felt most efficacious, such as my own experience in second grade of being the best swinger in the world at the park by my house where I could touch my toes to the leaves on the trees. It was like I was a bird and could fly. I try to find some experience like that in their past. Maybe they were good at art or piano or dancing or singing. Then I have them try to feel that same bodily feeling from that time in the past where they had control and were able to be and do in the world. I take them through all five senses, getting them to try to feel each one and then become aware of what thoughts those sensory images bring forth and understand what those thoughts are saying to the self. Those are important messages of wellness and healing and wholeness. At that point a lot of people open their eyes, and they can't believe they have that wholeness in them still, somewhere. Then I have them practice that twice a day so they can bring forth those feelings and thoughts at will. This gives a person a sense of safety where they can reside before returning to revisit the trauma.

In my own experience of somatic therapy, the very first thing I felt was literally the shock of what had happened when I was three. And the shock felt like I'd put my hand in an electric socket. I felt like my body was on fire. I was in genuine pain, and my throat was so constricted that I couldn't talk. That was my mutism. For me the somatic work was revisiting those things, and in the process I was able (with practice) to let go of the shock and feel my throat open up again.

It meant getting back my voice.

Be aware that it takes a lot of work to get to that point. Getting someone to feel safe in her own body can take numerous sessions. That's why it's so hard. I laugh when I think about it. Who goes into my field? Unstable people, right? I believe psychologists go into fields that illuminate our own traumatic experiences. Getting someone to feel safe in their own body is a start to healing.

It is important to find the things that are triggering them to have a fight or flight response, a panic attack, going mute—or even worse. Using the mindfulness I taught in the first step, I get them to concentrate on whatever images and sensations come up, then explore them more deeply. And at that point I usually find that people inevitably and naturally gravitate toward what I call the part that was missing: What needs to happen now that didn't happen then? An important fact for people to recognize is that the response they're having that's disrupting their lives is a response to something that's in the past. They have become stuck with a response to something that no longer exists. Obviously, if they're sitting in my office, they're not in the dangerous situation in which the trauma occurred; therefore, continuing to have the same response over and over again makes no sense any longer. At this juncture, I ask them, "What needs to happen now that didn't happen then?" It involves giving the frozen child part the attunement and nurturing it didn't get at the time of being a child. The adult self goes back to reclaim the lost child part. Once a person finds that missing piece of the puzzle, then they can feel efficacy again, and then all that fight or flight energy in the body gets discharged.

When we experience an overwhelming event, we have a physiological reaction, and an emotion follows. Then we tell ourselves a story about what happened and what this means about us. We get caught in these narratives, these internal working models that may become unthought knowns. We become so totally subsumed in our own stories of abandonment, betrayal, and/or loss, we are unable to stay connected to a greater reality. Trauma creates disconnection, and this may be the most painful loss of all—the loss of our connection to the Life Force itself, its pure love, and our very own soul. (There is an exercise in the back of the book that can help you make the connections, something you might like to try in your own healing journey.)

I like to think of this problem of having a fight or flight response as getting all dressed up with nowhere to go. The danger is long past, but the response gets stuck in the body. And then we develop symptoms because the body is under constant and unnatural stress. An animal in the wild also experiences these stresses and reacts with fight or flight responses. But when the danger passes, the animal doesn't keep reliving the danger. The panic is discharged through normal metabolism, and the animal goes back to a calm resting state.

When a human continues to relive the trauma, the symptoms that result from this stress can range from nervousness to anxiety, depression, and a whole range of physical symptoms, such as digestive trouble, backaches, headaches, and skin disorders. It can lead to autoimmune responses and to chronic illnesses such as Crohn's Disease, Addison's Disease, and irritable bowel syndrome.

Neurobiologists say that when we have an experience—any experience—it goes first to the body, and that means to the emotional system, because emotion involves feeling. We have the senses that process the experience, but they also label it as good, bad, or indifferent. But then with our big brains and our neocortex we immediately tell a story about what has happened, and that story comes to dominate, yet the story is almost always negative and probably wrong. It's the unthought known. And since the story takes over, our body can't do the natural thing. The natural process of discharging the stress gets thwarted.

I like to think of a zebra being chased by a lion. The zebra goes into a fight or flight response, charged with adrenaline, but if it escapes, it then starts shaking all over, discharging that energy. Robert Scaer, MD, ran the Mapleton Rehabilitation Center in Boulder, Colorado, and taught at the University of Colorado Health Sciences Center. In his book *The Trauma Spectrum*, he calls this discharge response, "a remarkable and relatively stereotyped pattern of movement that often resembles a grand mal seizure. There are many variations in this response, from relatively slight twitching movements to violent shaking . . . There are a number of names for this process, but the most accurate might be a *freeze discharge*." Peter Levine, a doctor of both biophysics and psychology, also found profound relief from PTSD in patients who were led through the process of freeze discharge through somatic therapy, which he teaches throughout the world.

The zebra can't tell a story about what happened because it doesn't have the brain power; it simply shakes and trembles until the experience is discharged and then goes on as if nothing happened. Of course, some learning takes place, and he may be quicker to run away next time, but as the neuroscientist Robert Sapolsky says, "Zebras don't get ulcers. If you get traumatized, you disembody. You live in your head. But that's where those stories are. And you're smart, so you think you can figure things out. But you can stay caught up there forever."

Patterns

I had a sixty-two-year-old client. Call him Jake. He had been seemingly happily married for more than thirty years when one day his wife said, "I hate you. I'm going to leave you." That shattered Jake's sense of his world, and he came to therapy. I very quickly picked up on the fact that he had what's known as the avoidant attachment pattern. If a mother ignores a baby's needs and fails to interact with him in a loving, caring way, the baby can grow into a person who does the same with any potential partners in his life. He won't attend to his wife's needs or respond to her in any emotionally satisfying way. And this produces the most painful sort of response. It turned out that when Jake was two years old, his mother had a baby who died. She fell apart and went into a mental hospital. His mother came out of the hospital a complete wreck and emotionally unavailable, leaving Jake to fend for himself. The result was that Jake was unable to connect emotionally with his wife and usually didn't recognize his own feelings. Mind you, this is a very smart man.

Working with me over the months, Jake gradually realized that when he was a little boy, his thinking went like this: *If I make mom mad, she'll die.* So I asked him to think that thought, and we tracked it somatically to see what would happen in his body. And then this amazing thing started to happen. He would take his arms, and he would try to lift them up. And he would feel all this pain in his arms, though he had no actual physical problems. At length we realized he was mimicking a toddler trying to reach up to be picked up. But he had lost his mobility because it was too frightening to reach up and get no response. To a small child, rejection is death. And I could completely empathize with that because of how my mother and grandmother had rejected me. Gradually, after numerous painful tries, Jake began to learn how to get that movement back. He began to experience genuine feelings and began to communicate with me more fully. I felt as if I were meeting a completely different person at that point. I call the somatic therapy that Jake experienced a miracle-producing approach because that's what Jake looked like once he was transformed: He looked like a miracle.

I have such a different quality of life because I went through that somatic process myself. I do it every day like a Zen meditation. And every day I practice mindfulness. As a result, I developed an ability to observe what I'm doing. I can observe my thoughts and feelings and sensations rather than being completely subsumed by them. To develop that capacity was profound. It was truly a lifesaving skill for me. The shock of trauma remains in the body until it's released. And until that's discharged, people who've been traumatized do not have the ability to speak up or push someone away. We just freeze all over again unless we practice.

It can also be helpful to get support from a spiritual healer in this quest. Somatic therapy can help us in the mental and physical aspects of our experience; deepening the spiritual connection, I believe, is the final piece of the puzzle—that mind-body-spirit connection. Just as we need helpers to regain a sense of psychological and physical well-being, we need spiritual guides to aid us to reconnect with our souls and the Life Force— the power of love energy. Melanie Davis-Jones has been one of those guides for me. (It is my luck she's also a writer who assisted with this book.) In 2013 Melanie did an intuitive energy healing for me that moved old, stuck energy that I had been holding onto since childhood. We did not revisit the traumas; it was a matter of recognizing my own spirit's ability to heal and releasing the energy around painful events. I was amazed at how I felt after one session—somehow lighter is the best way I can describe it. Her healings have greatly strengthened my connection to my own inner spirit and to the Life Force itself, helping propel me on my journey of healing.

In the old days it was thought that simply by talking about your trauma, you could get over it. But it turned out that talking about it before you were ready to talk would simply re-traumatize you. A person would relive the trauma, and that would show up in heart rate, blood pressure, skin conductance, and other measures of stress. Trauma therapy is not about remembering what happened. It's about processing it and integrating what happened so that, while the event is still there, you're not stuck in it. It's revisiting horrible events in people's lives, but you do it through sensation, and then the person does not get retraumatized. They say you "renegotiate" the trauma. I've seen it change lives completely.

My husband Harry is also a clinical psychologist, and I always find his ideas useful in dealing with trauma. He told me, "People come to therapy with three questions: Why do I do this? Why did I do that? And why do I keep doing this?" In other words, they keep doing something that seems beyond their will, contrary to logic and to their own well-being. And they have no idea why. "So part of the process," Harry said, "can be designed to uncover the motivating forces behind that." Precisely the work that he and I do. We delve deeply into the self to uncover the life experiences through the lens of which those destructive behaviors begin to make sense. And that becomes the platform from which those behaviors can be changed.

Harry told me about of one of his clients by way of illustrating how we may transcend that state in which we are doing things that baffle us, things that may not be in our best interest, things that send us to the psychologist to ask, "Why am I doing this?"

Harry's client was a man, but he liked to wear women's clothes. Call him Martin. One day Martin was in a department store shopping for clothes; he wore prosthetic breasts to complement the image of himself as a woman. On this particular day, Martin took a blouse into a fitting room to try on, but as he approached a cubicle one of the women nearby noticed he looked like a man. She told the salesperson who then called Security. The house detective came running to the rescue, and Martin was apprehended and exposed for the man he was. "He was embarrassed and criticized and yelled at and told to never come back to the store," Harry told me. "He came to see me because he's a white-collar professional, and his fear was that if they decided to arrest him for anything, he might lose his career. He's also married. And this really frightened him because his wife didn't know about his cross-dressing. He came in with a question: 'Why do I do this?' And also: 'I can't help it.'"

Over many therapy sessions it gradually came out that when Martin was a child, he had a nanny who would take him to the basement, dress him in girls' clothes, and fondle him. "And as he remembers this, he's feeling the gut experience of all that." Just as I've said, Martin began to feel his body doing what it had done during the childhood trauma. Harry began a course of what's known as EMDR, or Eye Movement Desensitization and Reprocessing, developed by

Francine Shapiro, PhD. It's a particular kind of somatic therapy that involves directing movements of the eyes while Martin recalled the traumatic events with the nanny. In Martin's case, after a number of sessions, he was able to recall in much greater detail exactly what happened to him as a child. As is common with EMDR, Martin began to view his childhood experiences more and more objectively, almost as if they had happened to someone else. That in turn had the effect of stripping the memories of their frightening emotional content.

One of the most interesting characteristics of Martin's case—in common with many others—is that at no time in his adult life as a cross-dresser did Martin make the connection with his childhood cross-dressing, even though they represented the same physical transformation of wearing the clothing of the opposite sex. Harry put it this way: "The unconscious mind is trying to resolve trauma by repeating the trauma and making it better somehow." But each time it doesn't get better, it merely results in more emotional pain. By working with Harry to objectify the events of his childhood and strip them of their toxic emotional associations, Martin was able to step away from that circular trap.

Harry explained to Martin that it's not possible to stop a compulsive behavior, but it is possible to replace it with another related behavior that might be better in some way. At the same time, over a period of time, Harry was giving Martin things to do outside the office. Harry would not prescribe or require the behaviors at first; rather, he would suggest or invite Martin to consider the behavior. For example, Martin kept his women's clothing in a chest in the attic to keep his wife from finding out. Harry suggested that he take the clothes and give them to Goodwill.

Harry told me, "Martin looked stricken and said, 'I don't think I can do that.'"

When Harry asked him why, Martin explained that when he felt the urge to walk through a department store dressed as a woman, he had to have a dress that fit him. And if he didn't have the dress and couldn't go to the department store, then the feeling would completely disable him. So Harry would get Martin to experience the disabling feeling by suggesting that he get rid of his clothes and then doing EMDR while Martin was still feeling that urgent compulsion and the fear of not being able to act on it. The EMDR lasted only a minute or two. Then Harry asked what feelings it brought up for Martin. He said he felt as if he were reliving the experience of walking down the basement stairs with the nanny, and that it was terrifying. As time went on, Harry would elicit that feeling in Martin and repeat the process, causing the intensity of the feeling to gradually decrease. In this way, Martin's initial panic at the idea of giving his wardrobe away diminished until gradually "I can't do it" became "Maybe I can do it," and then one day he said, "Yeah, I think I can do that." The process took months, but moving from impossibility to possibility is pretty powerful for someone in fear of losing his career. Mind you, this is not a judgment on Martin's wish to wear women's clothing. There's nothing morally wrong with cross-dressing. Morality wasn't Martin's concern. And he wasn't wearing women's clothing as a choice. His compulsion made him anxious and unhappy. Moreover, he lived in a society where cross-dressing might cost him his job. He felt he was in danger from himself, which is completely different from making a conscious choice about what clothes to wear.

Martin's dressing like a woman was not illegal, nor even objectionable in any absolute sense. Men dress like women all the time and vice versa. But Martin's fear of his own compulsion was disrupting his life. In addition, he was keeping a mammoth secret from his wife. The next step Harry took was to invite Martin to discuss his cross-dressing with his wife Dorothy. "I can't do that," Martin said emphatically.

"Well, what would that be like?" Harry asked. And Harry gently invited him to envision talking to her. How would he bring it up? What would the conversation be like? Did he trust her? Martin thought he did trust his wife, whom he felt knew him very well apart from the cross-dressing. Martin and Harry strategized about how he would tell his wife. And they concluded that the right way to go about it was for Martin to say, "Dorothy, I need you." And she would respond positively and offer to help. "What do you need?" she would ask. And then Martin would tell her he has an embarrassing problem.

"And he did tell her," Harry said. "And she was great." And this in turn gave rise to another discussion: Who cares if a man wants to wear women's clothing? What's important about clothing? Harry made the point that in our culture, we value free will and self-control. If a man decides to wear women's clothes, it is okay. But if he has an addiction or a compulsion, he is seen as not having self-control, and that is a source of shame. Our culture automatically shames those who succumb to compulsions—whatever the compulsion may be. And Martin knew that his cross-dressing was not a choice; it was a compulsion. Rather than practicing self-efficacy by cross-dressing, he was making himself a victim by being unable *not* to cross-dress.

Martin was able to short-circuit that compulsion by first getting rid of the clothing. Then he furthered his commitment by telling his wife, who was very supportive and helpful. And then Harry developed with Martin a menu of options to choose from when he felt the compulsion returning. One of them was to talk to his wife about the feeling. Another was to have a conversation with himself in which he expressed empathy for the little boy who was traumatized and understand what had happened to him. He would reassure himself that he was now grown up and could be okay. Another choice on the menu came from the fact that he loved music. He could turn to his music for self-soothing by playing an instrument and feeling the joy that arose from his ability and competence, his self-efficacy as a musician. He could rejoice in the knowledge that he had taken trauma and turned it into beauty simply by practicing. And the strategy worked pretty well, especially now that he had a companion who knew his secret, his wife Dorothy. He wasn't hiding anymore.

Harry was quick to point out that the consequences of early childhood trauma never go away. "With early trauma," he said, "the pathological behavior becomes the default behavior. Meaning that it's installed at our most vulnerable time of life, so it never goes away. Therefore, Martin has the potential to regress back to that compulsion under certain circumstances. As with any addiction, if he gets stressed out, if something bad happens, he can always go back to the old compulsion." That's why it's so important to replace the destructive behavior with constructive behaviors. That way he has something to fall back on whenever he feels the old urges overtaking him. In that way, the pathological behavior can become obsolete. Even though it doesn't vanish from the landscape of his mind and body, it no longer seems as relevant or satisfying as the new behaviors, which make him feel good about himself and his accomplishment in developing them.

As I said of my own response to trauma, it's not like it's totally eradicated. But I don't act on it anymore. And that's what Harry and I help people to achieve.

Harry

As I revisited my painful past to write this book, I began to feel sad and alone. Sometimes I didn't even want to go to work. I just wanted to stay with this and live inside it. I wanted to experience what I couldn't process when it was actually happening—to honor myself in that way. Somatic work helps us do now what we couldn't do when the trauma happened: stay *with* the sadness and sense of aloneness versus getting merged with it, making room for self-compassion and resolution. Sometimes I think I've used helping other people as an efficient distraction from facing my own problems. After Betsy died, I was a very different child. I was hypervigilant, focused on my mother's emotional cues. I couldn't explore and live carefree like a child is supposed to do. I couldn't develop my own life because I was so focused on attending to the threats around me. And of course, looming large among those threats was the possibility that my mother would kill herself if I didn't save her. I had seen her contemplate suicide at the bridge over the Fox River. If she had jumped with me in her arms, it would have been murder too. Maybe the next time she'd go without me and succeed. I had to watch her every minute.

I've often identified with characters in Stephen King's novels. I mentioned *The Shawshank Redemption*, which was made into a movie with Tim Robbins about a man wrongly convicted of a crime. Another one is *The Green Mile*, about a man on death row who takes on other people's suffering. As a result, he always feels tired and wants to be executed, even though he's been condemned for a crime that he didn't commit. Those two stories reminded me of myself before I learned how to become aware and change my behavior, change my thinking. You take on the suffering of other people, and then you're really exhausted, often not knowing why.

Before the age of three we don't remember things narratively because we don't have language. But we do remember them. Neuroscientists now believe that we remember everything. Memory is written in indelible ink; however, some things are written in invisible ink. We remember them somatically, not consciously. In other words, our bodies remember, as Porges says: neuroception. This is the unthought known. The body is on duty. And then, if the memories are formed by traumatic experiences, that same body begins to fall ill over time.

I can confirm what Harry said, though. You can get better, but it will take a long time. It takes intention and dedication. What I said earlier bears repeating. At the core of everything I've been working on is just how deeply, deeply alone I felt for most of my life. The condition I describe is profound. I can be surrounded by friends and family who love me, and I can still feel completely alone. But when I work at it, I can also come out of that. It wasn't until I was almost fifty years old that I was able to transcend those feelings. Today I don't feel that way anymore, and I'm not that way anymore. It's not easy to come out of isolation, yet after I made the transition, I felt really at peace with myself. All of a sudden when I made the transition I felt as if I were in the flow of life at last. After being stuck for so long, I felt like I belonged.

By the time I had escaped my abusive husband and had begun to study to be a psychologist, I had met Harry. He was one of my professors. I was taking my mother to chemotherapy for her ovarian cancer during the day and studying at night. Harry impressed me because he was kind. This was something that had been in short supply in my life. He was kind, and he was supportive. He seemed to really enjoy helping others. I recognized that I, too, had that same drive. It may have grown out of trauma—the desire to save my mother, to save my husband Jim—but helping is helping, and I knew that's what I wanted to do. It's the same reason I was driven to make this book come true. Because there truly is all that trauma out there—as we've experienced, especially through the pandemic—I want to do all I can to show people the path to release their burdens.

Harry and I married in 1996. At that time I was still far from finished with my struggle to become my true self. Harry was kind, and in that sense, I had chosen better than I had done before. But he had his baggage too. Who doesn't?

I have to admit that I didn't really want to marry Harry in the beginning. His family was quite troubled. There was not much food in the house, no heat in the St. Louis winters. Harry's mother was schizophrenic, and his father died when he was a freshman in high school, about the same age I was when my father died. That same year, Harry's mother had a lobotomy and was reduced to a vegetative state. Harry took care of her. We both took care of terribly broken mothers. Like knows like, I suppose.

In analyzing our marriage, I really think he had avoidant attachment issues, and I have anxious attachment issues. According to the attachment literature, that's a relationship made in hell. It worked like this: If I voiced a need, Harry took it as a demand. He wasn't good at discussing his feelings.

He got angry a lot. It wasn't a secure attachment, and this is sad because it was the best living situation I'd ever had. Most of all, though, it was lonely for me and must have been for him as well. I felt that I was not really there with him, nor was he able to really be there with me. We were like two children, clinging to each other, lost in the forest, when what we really wanted was just to be home. But there had never been a real home for either of us. I did not feel that we were connecting on a true heart-to-heart level. All that would change as Harry and I grew and worked on transformation. We had to start somewhere.

Part of Harry's issue with attachment resulted in him not including me completely in his life. For example, Harry's son from a previous marriage was going to marry a woman from Tanzania, and Harry was going to go to Africa for the wedding. He somehow neglected to invite me, even though I was his wife by that time. I was never included when it came to Harry's sons.

In February 2005 we were in Key West, and Harry was on the phone, making the arrangements for the wedding when I felt a snap in my heart. I got up and started to walk the eight miles around Key West. I was so upset. I was reliving the worst combinations, like my dad favoring my brother and my mom favoring my sister. In fact, when my father realized he was dying of cancer, he went to the Democratic Republic of the Congo to set up a hospital for charity. I was desperate to go with him, but he rebuffed me, saying that I was a girl, and it was more appropriate to take a boy. He took my brother instead. It took me some time to come to recognize that Harry's rejection of me was causing me to relive that experience, as well as the experience of my mother favoring Betsy. But another part of me was amazed, thinking, *The details are almost the same, and I'm going through it again!* And, of course, after a lifetime of experiencing therapy, both my own and that of others, I see now that this is an eternal pattern. We are destined to repeat what we don't understand.

I finally recognized that something was wrong with our marriage and that it needed attention. I had observed in my life that when one person decides to change, there's always the possibility that the people around them may not come along. Harry may not have wanted to change, which might have forced the two of us to part. Change is always risk, but I also understood that a failure to change could kill me. That snap in my heart wasn't imaginary. Psychological effects had done real physical damage in my life already. I knew I had to act.

Around that time, my family doctor heard a strange sound while listening to my heart. A follow-up with a cardiologist revealed a septal aneurysm. It was a broken heart. The cardiologist said it was benign and not to worry. Around Thanksgiving in 2004, a pediatrician discovered that my son Bobby was having heart issues of his own. The doctors said that one day in his thirties, Bobby would drop dead. Gratefully, that didn't happen, but this turned out to be another opportunity to connect with the Life Force, that pure love energy.

When we're open to it, we can see how somebody cares—I mean we can see how Spirit is working on our behalf. While I was attending a school meeting for a client, I needed to leave the meeting because Bobby's doctor was calling with his test results. Two holes were found in his heart. Unbeknownst to me, the father of my client had followed me out into the hallway and overheard the conversation. I was scared and worried about the next moves. By the time I got back to my office (a fifteen-minute drive), the father had called a contact he had at St. Louis Children's Hospital. As a result, Bobby was able to get the needed procedure done. The electrophysiologist who had orchestrated the procedure recommended I get an echocardiogram because these defects tend to run in families. I was a fifty-year-old woman, and the doctor ordered me to get an echo right then and there at a children's hospital! I could overhear a nurse grumbling that she was having to do the procedure on such an old person!

Lo and behold it was discovered through the echo that I was in serious heart failure. It confirmed my septal aneurysm. I also had a severely leaking mitral valve, four arrhythmias, and an injection fraction so low that I was almost at the point of needing a heart transplant. The doctor told me that one day I'd just stand up and not be able to walk across the room. I wasn't experiencing any pain, and there wasn't a history of heart problems in my family, so I had no idea. I was short of breath, and I was tired a lot, but I just thought I worked too much, when actually I had about six weeks to live!

If the father hadn't eavesdropped on my conversation with Bobby's doctor, *if* we didn't have the doctor we did for Bobby, *if* he hadn't ordered the echo, etc., I wouldn't be here today. Sometimes I wonder how often we miss (or dismiss as coincidence) these synchronistic cues from the Universe that are there to help us and let us know we are not alone.

By May 2005, right after Harry and I were in Key West, I was in the hospital having open heart surgery. And my intention was, as soon as I recovered from the surgery, to get a divorce. By then I was aware that the family dynamics of being excluded from contact with Harry's sons was actually killing my heart, as I was forced to relive the rejection and abandonment of my own childhood. I had to save my own life or die. The Life Force helped me get in a state of gratitude.

When I found out I needed to have open heart surgery, of course I was frightened and upset, yet in preparation, I understood the importance of getting my body into as positive a state as possible. I would learn much more about the neurobiology of this later on, but I did know enough to know that getting my body out of the fear state as much as possible was my responsibility so the doctors could do their part.

Twelve people planned to be in the waiting room as I had my surgery. For each of them I prepared a gift bag that contained headphones with three of my favorite songs: "What a Wonderful World," "Somewhere Over the Rainbow," and "In This Life." I wrote thank-you notes titled "100 Ways I Know God Loves Me" to my family, Harry, Sarah, and Bobby to express my thankfulness for the love and joy they had brought to me. I had accepted I might not survive the surgery, and I felt deeply grateful for the many chances life had brought me to heal. That felt like a victory itself.

I nearly died, and I knew it. Moreover, I knew I did not want to die. Sometimes people accept death, welcoming it as a relief from suffering, but I really wanted to live for so many reasons: my children, my practice, even for Harry. And of course, for life itself. I looked at myself, and I saw these patterns of self-negation that are so deeply ingrained in me that I knew I had to change myself. I realized that when someone was mistreating me, and I couldn't speak up about it, I would become physically ill from the stress and internal conflict.

To his credit, Harry was able to recognize how unhealthy the patterns we both carried were, and he went along with my plan to change. We went to therapy. We worked together, and we worked it out, little by little.

Lineage

In the aftermath of my surgery and in the course of working my life out with Harry, I began to think more and more about where it all started with my family. Certainly my mother wasn't born in hell. She was not a devil. She was a woman and had once been a baby too, an innocent and undamaged child. What had happened? I began to think about Joan's German mother, my grandmother, Marguerite Heineman. Joan's grandfather came over from Germany at the age of sixteen. His father had told him, "If you don't make it, just kill yourself. Don't come back." The boy had been apprenticed to a photographer in Germany, so when he got to Chicago, he set up a camera on a street corner. He worked seven days a week and saved his pennies and gradually worked his way up to having a good photography studio of his own. He lived upstairs from the studio with my great-grandmother, who also came from the old country as an orphan. There was plenty of trauma going back at least four generations.

Knowing how history is, it probably went back a lot further. My great-grandfather died when I was eight. He seemed like a kind soul. Trauma doesn't always make bad dogs. It can make docile dogs too. Perhaps my great-grandfather was one of those.

But my great-grandmother—Marguerite's mother—was quite the other end of the spectrum. If she got mad at you, she wouldn't talk to you for a couple weeks. The mute theme runs in my family. My great-grandparents had two girls, and one of them was Marguerite. I think about her, and my brain gets confused. Even now, I can scarcely talk about my grandmother. When Marguerite gave birth to my mother's sister, she spent six weeks in the hospital. When she didn't want to deal with the world, she would go to the hospital. She would go up to the Mayo Clinic when things were happening in the family.

I truly believe Marguerite was one of those evil ones that the psychiatrist Scott Peck, MD, describes in his book *People of the Lie*. In one story from the book, a family has a child who dies by suicide with a gun. The next Christmas, the parents give that gun to the other son as a gift. That's what Marguerite was like. My mother and my aunt were terrified of her. She could give you a withering look that would chill your blood.

When my son Bobby was little, he was fidgeting and accidentally bumped his foot against Marguerite's leg.

And whoa! The look she gave him. I realized that's what we'd all been afraid of. It was annihilating.

Marguerite would do things such as this: "Is anyone hungry?" Which translated to: "I'm hungry."

I'd say, "Okay, let's get something to eat."

"Well, where would you like to go?" Marguerite would ask.

"How about Charlie Trotter's?"

"Do you really want to go *there*?"

Everything was covert with her. Everything was manipulative. She could never simply say what she wanted. You had to read her. And you'd just better have the right answer. People like that can't get out of themselves to show up for someone else. She was like the evil villain in a movie. Frankly, if you put her in a movie, people would think you were exaggerating.

When I was in my early thirties, I was trying to piece together the story of what had happened to our family because no one ever talked about anything. Betsy's name was literally not mentioned, except for my mom telling me she was the pretty one. I went to my grandmother and asked her what had happened the day of Betsy's funeral. Marguerite turned icy cold and wrote me a letter that she never sent. I found it after her death. It said, "Tell Connie that her asking me about Betsy's death was the worst thing that's ever happened to me in my life." She had paper-clipped the letter to her will.

Marguerite had a killer look. She wouldn't yell, but her intensely angry demeanor could stop you cold. My mother lived in St. Louis when she got sick with ovarian cancer. My grandmother was still in Chicago, not terribly far away. I know my mom avoided contact with her for a reason. My mom's condition always worsened when Marguerite came to visit.

One time we had this incredible reenactment in my mom's kitchen. It was the three of us: my mom, my grandma, and me. Just like that day on the top of the stairs after Betsy's funeral. Only this time it was my grandma who was upset because my mom was dying. I actually remember thinking, *Should I do to her what she did to me? Rebuff her?* Instead, I gave her a hug. All I remember is that after my mom died, my grandma asked me if I would return to her a bathrobe that she had recently given my mom as a gift. She wanted it back, not for sentimental reasons. It was like my mom had no significance to her. It was beyond coldhearted.

When I talk about my grandmother, it's so distressing that I feel as if I stop making sense and become incoherent. I can forgive my mother and father and even Jim. But my grandmother? I believe she meant to hurt us; I saw it the most in how she treated Joan. One of the things that made it hard for me to stay in the world was my grandmother, who wanted people tangled up, especially if you dared to assert yourself. That's what made things so unbearable for me. If my mom dared to assert herself, her mother would know just the right thing to say to immobilize her.

Perhaps the worst thing about my position, not to mention Betsy's, was how irrelevant we both were to the war between Joan and Marguerite. I see that now. Betsy's death and my trauma were just collateral damage in the war between those two women. That's why I related to Andy Dufresne in *The Shawshank Redemption*. Imprisoned but innocent.

As badly as my mom was treated and as badly as she treated us, it still didn't feel malevolent. I know it sounds contradictory because she told me she wanted to break my will, and she told me she wanted us to be scared of her. But there still was something qualitatively different about my grandmother. And I'm still at a loss to explain where that malevolence came from. Marguerite's parents were well off and seemed to have a good relationship. I have no evidence of trauma in my grandmother's background that may have distorted her personality so badly, although it's certainly possible that it happened and she simply never talked about it. The most likely source was her mother's rejections. Are some people born evil? It seems unlikely to me. I believe that something had to have happened to her to twist her in that way. Whatever it might have been has faded into mist.

When I was a sophomore in high school, not long after my father died, I thought, *We're in trouble now*, being left with mom. One night before I went to bed, I had to read Wordsworth's "Ode: Intimations of Immortality from Recollections of Early Childhood" for school. I had been moved to think that I could lose everything in the blink of an eye, as my father had. What's the point in going on? What can you count on? Because of my traumatic losses, I knew that I could lose everything in the blink of an eye. "What's the point of going on?" I asked, "God! Dad! Are you out there? Where are you?"

When I slept that night, I experienced a vision. In it, I was brushing my waist-length hair in front of my bedroom mirror. I heard the front door open and close. I ran to the landing at the top of the stairs (the exact spot Betsy had ingested the medicine) and saw my dad standing at the foot of the stairs. He was wearing a powder-blue sweatshirt that said "The University of Heaven." I yelled, "Dad! Dad! How are you?!" He said, "I'm fine. The tests are hard, but I got my degree." I woke up and had the sense that what had happened had a different quality than a dream. It felt as though my spirit was directly communicating with my dad's spirit. And from that, I gained a clear sense, a knowing, an epiphany, that the one thing that no one can take away from you is the way you choose to respond to a situation. You can respond constructively or destructively. That's all you ever have and all you ever need.

As Viktor Frankl said in *Man's Search for Meaning*, he could not change the fact that he was in Auschwitz, but he alone controlled his internal response to that situation. In that sense, he remained free even while imprisoned.

Most people take their traumas to their graves. And I don't know if they have any conscious knowledge of how they diminished their lives. For a lot of people it takes them to an early grave because trauma causes physical damage. It almost took me to an early grave, except for all the work I've done to heal.

When I said, "It should have been me who died, not Betsy," things got better between me and my mother for a time. And indeed, Joan began to set some minor boundaries on Marguerite as well, not catering to her quite as much. My grandmother noticed and did not like that at all. She wanted to come down to St. Louis to visit when Joan was diagnosed. Joan said it wasn't a good time for her to visit, and Marguerite said, "Well, you know, Joan, when I was on the way to the hospital to deliver you, a black cat crossed my path, and that's why your life has been cursed."

Even though things had gotten better between me and my mom, whenever my grandma did something like that, I'd lose my mother to that dark place again. She'd become lost in her own drowning well of pain. Marguerite had the ability to completely crush her daughter whenever she chose to do so, especially when my mom stood up for herself and didn't cave in to Marguerite's iron will. This was the drama I saw played out my entire life. I was always in the eye of the storm.

Good-Bye

At the time that Joan was diagnosed with ovarian cancer, I was just leaving Jim and planning to go back to graduate school. Marguerite scolded me for not helping my mother more, even as I took Joan to chemotherapy in the day and went to school at night while taking care of two children. My grandparents had money. They could have helped my mom. Marguerite was the kind of person who, if you were having any joy at all, she would want to destroy it. At the abject horror of my grandmother's personality, I would often fall into silence, just sitting and heaving huge sighs, finding myself unable to speak.

My mother was obviously extremely cruel and did tremendous damage. And my mom even intended to hurt us because she herself was hurting. But she didn't plot it out. I believe in my heart that my grandmother knew, she plotted, she thought about what to say to do the most damage to us. In psychological terms her behavior would be called "malevolent." She actually wanted to destroy life.

On the day of Joan's funeral, after she had succumbed to ovarian cancer, my grandmother was talking and laughing outside the church. Then she walked into the church with an inappropriate mink coat on. When she saw me, she tried to look sad. Everything was an act with her. Everything was a narcissistic injury to her. At the funeral, she again mentioned the bathrobe that she had given my mom as a gift. She said she wanted it back because Joan didn't really appreciate it enough.

The last time I ever saw my grandmother, I was in Chicago for a trauma conference of all things. About ten years had elapsed since my mom died. I was at The Drake Hotel. Marguerite lived down the street. I hadn't seen her for years. Things were very different by that time. I had evolved out of the depths into a successful professional. I was my own person. Marguerite lived on Lake Shore Drive, so I walked the few blocks to her building, and the maid let me in.

Children can't understand everything, but they can store things away and take them out to examine them in the later light of adult learning. I still needed to know what had happened to me and Betsy and the family during that terrible time so long ago. I needed to shed some light on the calamity that had shaped my life and tortured me so—the light of my life, my salvation and only friend, gone in a terrible instant. And here was the one person left who could do that: Marguerite. As soon as she saw me, the first words out of her mouth were, "Can't you just let this go?" I knew in that moment I wouldn't get anywhere with her.

I leaned over and gave her a kiss on her cheek and said, "Godspeed, Grandma. I wish you well." And I knew in my heart that would be the last time I'd ever see her.

I had begun to try to figure out what was wrong with my family, and I had naively expected people to rally around me and try to work toward being more authentic with one another. Marguerite took what I did as an attack on her. She could tell when I was around her that I had gotten stronger and wasn't fawning over her the way everybody else did. I left the condominium very quickly after that last meeting, unable to stand being around her any longer. When I went to Marguerite's funeral a few years later, I saw that there was absolutely no grief in that room. Like many such people, disconnected from the feelings of others, Marguerite lived to a very old age, 104.

As a consequence of all this self-examination, I look back on the day of Betsy's funeral and think about how desperate I must have been to turn to my grandmother and ask to live with her. If she had said yes, it probably would have killed me. It certainly would have been worse than living in my own home. Of course, I was only three and could not have known.

Perhaps it was my grandfather who saved something in my persona that gave me the strength to live. I loved my grandpa, although he was a man given to rages and limited affection. Both his parents came from Poland. He came from great poverty; he had no shoes as a child. To change his life, he changed his name from Cylkowski to Sill and started his own construction company. He was hardworking and made a success of his company. I loved him, but he was never able to express himself to me. When my father died, he took the family on a vacation to Mackinac Island as a gesture, but he was never able to offer condolences to me or my family.

In those days, to get into Duke University, a prospective student had to visit the school for an interview in person. Of course, my mother wouldn't take me, so my grandfather did. But we visited only the engineering school, and I didn't get to see where I'd live, something I really cared about. I wound up feeling that he was completely out of touch with me, even as he was trying to do something generous. He, too, had been frozen by his childhood trauma—frozen and mute. I felt that we were reaching for each other across an unbridgeable distance.

At the time that my grandfather died, I was still married to Jim and living on Whidbey Island near the Navy base. No one from the family told me that my grandfather had died until the funeral was over. "We didn't want to bother you," Marguerite said. It was a vicious stroke of revenge for the affection between me and my grandfather. I could scarcely believe that even Marguerite could do such a thing. In truth I was hardly surprised. There's something about people where you can feel that they have a spark inside despite their outward expression. I feel like my grandfather did. Trauma can be transmitted down through the generations by behavior like this. But I believe health can be transmitted too. If one generation works to break the negative patterns, then the next generation can break them too. Energy healers say that an individual's healing allows for healing seven generations forward and back. (Seems like a good reason for us to do the work!)

My mother was diagnosed with ovarian cancer within two months of me putting my foot down and setting limits on her behavior. I wasn't letting my mom do to me what her mom had done to her. At that point in her life she could have examined herself and what her mom had done to her. I believe that it was easier for her to die than to do all that work on herself.

Having the mom I did, I'm super-attuned to people —too attuned. It makes me very attuned to my clients, but sometimes it's exhausting. I can see, for example, that my grandmother was relieved when my mom died. She didn't seem sad at all.

My grandfather, Vincent "Sill" Cylkowski, explained to me that he was going to make a trust that would divide his money upon his death among the six grandchildren: Joan's four children and her sister's two children. There were separate arrangements for Marguerite. They lived very well. They had a place in Arizona for the winter. They'd go to Switzerland for Christmas.

With both my dad and my mom I can see from where I am now that everyone was so unconscious, they were like marionettes on strings acting out their pain and pathology. With my grandmother, it was *if* you're happy, I'm going to make you feel bad. That malevolence was palpable and terrifying. There's a difference between impulsively being hurtful and then being sorry for it and those who plot their evil and deliberately commit it and have no remorse. It makes me see now, with deep sadness, how much of a victim my mother was.

Self-Love

I stopped eating in the seventh grade. My grandfather made Marguerite take me to Florida. I guess he thought it would help, but I still wouldn't eat. I don't think I had body image issues, really. I think it was my way of screaming out to people that I was in pain. Like when I dressed as a broken heart for Halloween; again, I just couldn't express it with words. I got really, really skinny, but then I had an attack of appendicitis and had to go into the hospital. They told me to eat, and I did. I don't think I had anorexia. I simply wanted attention and wasn't getting it. And I was in that transition age from little kid to teenager when acting out is common.

I think my mom, overall, did better than her mom. And that's kind of pathetic, given my mom. I felt as if I failed my kids initially because I was in such an abusive situation with Jim. The kids had to witness that violence. I remember a moment with Sarah when Jim and I were in a screaming match. She was probably around four or five. I saw the terror in her eyes. I saw that look. I'll never forget it, but I chose not to address it with her. Upon reflection and tons of years of agony, I can show some compassion for myself. This is an important part of the process of healing. You have to learn to love yourself, have compassion for yourself, and forgive yourself. Self-love is the ultimate goal of psychotherapy and spiritual work—having a transcendent sense of yourself aligned with, and an expression of, the Life Force, connecting with pure love of self. I didn't address it with Sarah because I didn't yet have the means to do anything about it. I couldn't leave Jim because I didn't have the money. I felt completely trapped. I felt that going back to my mom's was worse than being with Jim. None of this was cognitive; it was simply a decision that was made unconsciously. So now I have to look back and see that young mother as someone struggling helplessly to get out. I finally did just that.

I spent at least twenty-five years getting us out and making amends. It caused a big problem between me and Sarah. For a time, she felt about me the way I felt about my mom. She felt like she had to be good so I would stay regulated. After years of therapy and hard work, I've changed the patterns, and at last it feels like the cycle is really over. Sarah and I are very close now, and we have secure attachment, but it was a long road to get here. I can see the residual damage, but I believe that both Sarah and Bobby are fulfilling their own dreams now. Bobby grew up to become a physician, and Sarah has a job with a major international art museum.

She had her first baby in 2014, and I feel like everything that needed to be said has now been said. Sarah and I spent about ten years talking about how much I suck. She has had a tough time balancing her ability and willingness to listen and change with the impulse to dissolve into helpless shame and paralyzing guilt. I feel like it's amazing, though, because the three of us are so close now. That's what I call a hard-work miracle.

To them I passed along the tenets of the unthought known and how we can transcend them. There are times in our lives in which we experience the peace of our essential selves. It may be just a glimpse, but sometimes we can be released from the fight/flight/freeze response and actually feel free. Be in the flow state. Sarah felt it in the undercroft of the Canterbury Cathedral; Bobby while skiing in the Teton mountains; me while swinging in the neighborhood park. At the end of this book, we share a method by which to intentionally bring this into our experience to invite you into the feeling—that time of connection to something greater than ourselves and our individual outward identities.

I believe now that no matter how insecurely attached you were as a child, you can have secure attachment with your children by working hard. It's called "earned attachment." With it, you can not only heal yourself, but you can be a better parent and prevent the trauma from penetrating to the next generation.

As I became more and more sensitive to signs from the Life Force/God/the Universe, I directly asked my spirit to send me a sign that was beyond coincidence. Something I couldn't second-guess.

Part of my daily morning ritual was to say these words: "I say yes to letting go. I say yes to aligning myself to the Life Force." I asked for some sign to let me know I was on the right path, that I could trust my spirit, not just my old survival patterns. As I was reading my emails one morning, up popped a website titled The YES Necklace! How could I dispute that sign? I ordered six of them!

Sugarplum

When I was a toddler, my grandmother gave me a book called *Sugarplum*, written by Johanna Johnston and published in 1955. It is about a tiny doll. Because she's so small, the other dolls think she's "a trinket, a bangle, or a knickknack, and not a *real* doll at all."

Bad things happen to Sugarplum. She falls out of her owner Suzie's pocket. She gets lost on the playground at school; a bird finds the doll and returns her. Then Sugarplum falls behind the bureau. Lost and nearly forgotten, she is sucked up by a vacuum cleaner. Luckily, a penny is sucked up with Sugarplum, and the cleaning lady empties the bag to find it. Once again, Sugarplum is returned to Suzie.

Through all her travails, Sugarplum wished for real doll clothes. She was a carved doll, and her clothing was merely painted on. She thought that if only she could have the frills and ribbons that real dolls wore, then the big dolls would recognize her for what she was: different but a real doll. Every time Suzie tried to make her clothes, the girl became frustrated at her lack of skill and quit.

Back on the shelf with the other dolls, Sugarplum suffers humiliation at their hands, but she keeps up her hope. Her mantra is "I *am* a real doll. I *am*. I *am*."

Then one day Suzie's mother is making jelly, and Sugarplum falls into a jar. The jelly cools and coagulates. Sugarplum is stored away in the basement among all the other jars. You can hardly tell she's there in that murky rose-colored jam. Sugarplum loses heart. As the days stretch into weeks, Sugarplum begins to admit the reality of her being: "I guess I can't be much more than a trinket, a bangle, or knickknack, for whoever heard of a *real* doll getting lost in a glass of jelly? The big dolls were right."

The illustration of her stuck in a jelly jar in the dark basement is a great representation of a child who is immobilized and mute as a result of trauma. In the essay "Sketch of the Past," the novelist Virginia Woolf, who was severely abused as a child, described this state as a feeling "of lying in a grape and seeing through a film of semi-transparent yellow." It was dissociation, the complete loss of feeling, that Woolf describes as "this cotton wool, this non-being. Week after week passed at St. Ives [her childhood summer home] and nothing made any dint upon me" in the article "Moments of Being." It reminds me of me.

After a very long time in the exile of the basement,

Suzie's mother picks that very jar of jelly to bring upstairs into the light. When she pops the paraffin seal and turns the jelly out onto a plate, she exclaims, "For goodness' sake!" and hurries up the stairs to bring the jelly to her daughter, saying, "Maybe that will make Suzie smile a little, at last!"

It turns out that in Sugarplum's absence, Suzie has grown sick and lethargic. Her mother brings the jelly upstairs. Suzie lies in bed, too weak to take much interest, but when she sees that Sugarplum is embedded in the jelly, she begins to laugh. The big dolls say, "Suzie's laughing at last. Now she'll get better. And it's Sugarplum's doing!" They conclude, "Why, she must be a sort of a doll, after all."

Then Suzie's mother helps her make a tiny dress for Sugarplum. "It was a perfect little dress, and Sugarplum's own!"

"Sugarplum's a *real* doll," cry all the big dolls.

"And," writes Johnston, "because of the sash Suzie tied round her middle, she never got lost again."

My grandmother gave me that book when I was nearly two and Betsy was eight months old. It always seemed so odd to me that a book with such significance came from her. Her refusal to aid in my escape when I was three was what cast me into profound trauma. Like being in the jelly jar, that was my life. Interesting that my grandmother, who could have saved me from the "jelly jar," gave me a children's book about immobilization, depression, and redemption. At four or five years of age I drew circles or mandalas on the very last page.

Mandalas are symbols of wholeness, completion. They are thought of as symbols of transforming suffering into joy and happiness. Something in my subconscious mind knew I would take this journey, the hero's journey, from trauma to transcendence.

Joseph Campbell, who studied comparative mythology, describes the journey of the archetypal hero. The hero receives a calling; she can accept or refuse it. If she refuses, she maintains the status quo or may even regress. If she accepts the calling, the hero faces many obstacles that are actually necessary for growth. Along the way, the hero meets allies, either human or spiritual. As it is for Frodo and Sam in *The Lord of the Rings*, the journey is long and treacherous. Yet at the end the hero finds a great treasure. That treasure is the authentic self: the soul. That is what Sugarplum found: a sense of her higher self. Being a real doll.

I began to feel like a "real doll" only when I started to use my voice. Although I had been assertive before that, after my first surgery in 2005, I trusted myself in a new way. Previously if someone overrode me, I'd usually go mute again, but I learned if I kept my ground and had requirements in my relationships, I was able to keep people from bulldozing right over my feelings. It was coming out of immobilization that I began to experience myself as a real person. Moving up the scale to social engagement.

When you're traumatized, you have a dual reality. One part of you acts like nothing happened, and another part of you acts like it never stopped happening. I had a belief early on that I was so irrevocably broken that I just didn't belong. I was wrong. There's hope for everyone if it can work for me. I tell my clients, "I'm your personal trainer for your brain." I literally help them get their bodies into a state of arousal similar to the one they experienced during trauma. Then I gradually let them change their relationship with that bodily state. This somatic therapy is able to create the new learning that dismantles the old beliefs. I tell my clients, "We're going to retrain your brain, and it takes practice and repetition, but you really can do it."

Recently I revisited the Sugarplum jelly jar. I believe it is the ultimate happy ending to a story of transcendence. Like the phoenix rising from the ashes. I believe that most people can do this process safely in therapy, but I actually got to reenact the whole thing in real life when I was attacked during my group therapy session and suffered broken heart syndrome and wound up in the hospital once again. That was not my conscious intention, to be sure. Nevertheless, it happened, and I now proudly live to tell the tale so you may feel inspired to take that first step toward healing, the way to living your own truth and being a "real doll!"

Epilogue

While I was in the process of finishing this book, I experienced another life-altering connection with the Life Force/God/the Universe. It was too profound to leave it out of what I have chosen to share with you. I call it my "MRI miracle."

You'll recall that when I had the near-death experience at the age of three, I felt the terrible physical pain of shock—sharp, life-threatening pain that felt like getting electrocuted. When I returned to my body, the pain was waiting for me. I couldn't speak for an entire year. I was too scared to talk. I was trapped in my own body, my own world.

As a consequence, feeling trapped has been a persisting terror of mine. Overcoming the feeling of a total lack of control and gaining the ability to act on one's own behalf has been a lifelong process . . . one that was put to the test in the spring of 2022.

It was discovered that my heart was going into

ventricular tachycardia (V-tach), and my doctors wanted to do further exploration. With the many heart-related procedures I've had over the years as part of my heart recovery saga, I've had several CT scans but never a cardiac MRI. Upon arrival at the hospital, the technician told me cardiac MRIs are the most difficult in that they last an hour, and you can't move your shoulders or hips because if you do, you have to start over. It is cold and loud and downright unpleasant. What I didn't connect was that having this test would engender the same feeling of being immobilized and trapped, until I was buckled in on the gurney and slid into the machine. I was given a bulb I could press if I couldn't endure the test.

Inside the machine with the loud noise and cold blasts, I considered having a meltdown and refusing the test, but that really wasn't an option because scar tissue was causing my heart to go into V-tach, a life-threatening condition that can cause the heart to stop. My doctors needed this MRI to decide how best to proceed with my care. I realized I had to find a way to endure the test.

Then my brain remembered all the training I had done to learn to calm my body and mind. I relaxed my body. Then I did my mindfulness practice to quiet the fear thoughts that were screaming in my head. My body started to calm, but then there was the terribly scary moment when I could actually feel my heart go into the V-tach. But I could also feel the ability I had developed to go into an observing and compassionate part of me—

that is, to observe what was happening to me dispassionately and send myself loving kindness. I could let go of the outcome. My fear thoughts were focused on how many beats in V-tach would kill me and how many would allow me to survive. I was able to let this go and be present to the experience. Whatever happened.

There in the machine, it occurred to me that this was what had happened to me at the age of three. My heart stopped because of shock. Of course, at three I had no ability to be mindful. I was fully hijacked by the experience. It had its way with me. It had subsumed me. Was I getting some strange opportunity for a redo? Could I reexperience that terrifying event and this time renegotiate my relationship to terror and feeling trapped? I truly think so.

Each and every time a V-tach event occurred during the hour in the MRI machine, I would relax and, in a sense, watch it instead of relive it. Then something remarkable happened. I heard what sounded like a heartbeat other than mine: *Lub dub. Lub dub. Lub dub.* The technician told me later that this was the sound of the equipment and its cooling system, but for me, when I could quiet my body and mind, it felt like my heart and the heart of the Life Force were unified. My little human heart was being supported by the pure love and power of the Life Force itself. I couldn't hear or feel or acknowledge that incredible presence when I was paralyzed in fear. Only when I could relax could I take in the whole of the experience.

I was reliving my near-death experience, but this

time I was able to stay present and aware of the experience. This time I surrendered to the outcome. I didn't feel trapped; I felt empowered, whole, and loved. A victory! As I was able to quiet my fear and hear the heart of God, the Life Force, and feel the pure love, a deep comfort enfolded me, and this thought arose like a mantra: *Love comes for me.* Yes, love comes for me. It was like being enfolded in an ineffable comfort and warmth, not unlike the angel coming for me in the near-death experience. To me that is the lesson: to open our hearts, knowing that pure love is ever-present. When we move out of our own way, and from a posture of receptivity, healing comes for us; compassion comes for us; love comes for us all.

The exercise at the end of this book is a beautiful way to start to reconnect with yourself and find a way to deepen your connection to healing, compassion, and love.

Resource

The need for access to mental health support has skyrocketed in recent years, so it felt important to add something that has worked for me personally.

The following methodology is one approach you might use as a contemplative practice; it deepens the mind/body/spirit connection by taking the somatic therapy I do with my clients and adding some techniques from an intuitive meditation practice to create an uncomplicated approach that can become part of your daily practice. We offer it as an option to have you consider and explore what feels right for you.

METHODOLOGY | Recentering: Coming Back to Ourselves

In the 1990s a discovery was made in neuroscience called "neuroplasticity": the ability of the brain to rewire itself. This opened up a whole new world for trauma recovery. We *can* relearn new responses to old triggers. Some neuroscientists separated a basketball team: one group actually doing free throws, the other visualizing them. When they got the team together, those who actually practiced were only marginally better than those simply imagining it. The same exercise was done with pianists: one doing, one imagining. Same results.

In studying why this is so, neuroscientists discovered when we imagine, our brain and nervous systems don't know the difference from actually performing an action, but our minds know the difference and can redirect themselves.

Think of it this way. You're feeling neutral, and a song or photo reminds you of a happy time. Nothing changed in what you were doing, but emotional memory kicks in, and you feel happy; the body remembers as well. Where the mind goes the body follows.

We can use this power to our advantage; we can use it consciously. The following exercise combines the somatic practice I frequently use with my clients with intuitive energy healing techniques (shared by my friend Melanie). Together they support body, mind, and spirit. I invite you to try. (Yes, it's easier if you record the steps and play them back until you're familiar with the process.)

- Let's begin by closing your eyes, if you're comfortable, and taking a few deep breaths, in through the nose, out through the mouth. As

you feel your body starting to relax, use the rhythm of your breath to set your intentions. On the exhale, release (stress, anxiety, tiredness . . . whatever you choose); on the inhale, set the intention to breathe in pure love.
- Now imagine there are roots at the bottom of your feet and gently visualize those roots going down into the center of the Earth. Go as deep as feels comfortable, then imagine something the roots can attach to: boulders, gems, tree branches . . . whatever comes to you. This level of grounding will help your body feel centered and stabilized. The more grounded we are, the more our spirits can come into our bodies to support our healing.
- Next, think of a state of mind-body that you'd like to be your baseline: joy, peace, confidence, etc. Then think of a time in which you experienced that. (For me as a woman in my fifties, when I was asked when I felt peace, it was swinging in second grade.) Use a memory or one that approximates it.
- Now bring that image up and make it as clear as possible in your mind like you're looking at a photograph.
- Then imagine that you could take your attention and put it in an elevator and go deep down into your body.

- Imagine yourself looking around and imagine how your body experiences this physiological state. Do you notice your heart rate, breathing, muscles, or energy somewhere? Put your focus there, and notice you're not in thought or emotion; you're in the body.
- Ask yourself these questions (with the five senses): Is there a color? Sound? Taste? Texture? Temperature? (warm, cool, or neutral)
- Now let's imagine that this sensation/good feeling has words of wisdom for you. It may have a message of something it wants you to know and trust. Perhaps it does or it doesn't; either is okay. Remember there's no wrong way to do this; it is your unique experience.
- Then let's imagine we could put you on a raft in not a body of water but rather what you selected as your baseline: peace, confidence, or whatever state of mind you've chosen to work with.
- Imagine your arms and legs dangling off the sides and you're a sponge absorbing this sensation/feeling. If your body gave you a word or phrase, repeat the word(s) slowly ten times.
- Now imagine the energy of that same sensation beaming down on you through the top of your head like the warmth of sunshine, fully infusing you with this positive state from

below and above. You're giving your nervous system a vacation, and you soak this in until you can't take in another drop.
- Take a few deep cleansing breaths as you state the current date and your present age. Send gratitude to your body, mind, and spirit for the support during the exercise.

Ideally, practice this for five to ten minutes twice a day, but remember, don't beat yourself up if you miss a day or two, or even a week. Simply get back to the practice as best as you can. There's no place for judging ourselves or letting others dissuade you from your practice. This is *your* healing journey.

Disclaimer: This practice is only intended to elicit a more relaxed state in the body, not as a therapeutic tool. If any aspect of this practice is triggering or overwhelming, refrain from continuing and seek professional help. If you have experienced trauma or extreme stress, find a therapist who uses trauma-informed practices and is skilled in the techniques.

Acknowledgments

Creating a book that may be helpful to someone has been a lifelong dream. As a child I went to books, not my parents, to find answers for what I may be seeking. I always found answers there. My wish is that this book might do the same for someone who feels as alone as I once did.

To bring this dream to fruition, I have been blessed by the generosity of many.

First and foremost, I wish to thank my family. My husband, Harry, for his endless encouragement and varied technical help. And I am grateful to my children, Sarah and Bobby, for allowing me to expose our story. This took courage on their part.

To many of my clients who have encouraged me along the way. I am so appreciative of your support and belief in me. To the many friends who have loved me and supported me on this more than a decade long journey, I appreciate you.

To Stephen Porges who has given me such unwavering support for the last twenty years. (He would return my emails within five minutes!) His generosity of time and wisdom, as evidenced in the Foreword he wrote for the book, will always stand out as one of the deepest acts of kindness I've experienced in my life.

To Dr. Craig Reiss, my cardiologist, without whom I wouldn't be here to get the chance to tell my story.

To Mike Jaudes who helped me so early on to reenter and love my body.

And to my dear friend, Sean O'Brien, who is not here to see the results of his kindness, but without whom I wouldn't have made it.

To Melanie Davis-Jones, without her love and her writing acumen, this book would never have reached completion. We connected over twenty years ago and I remember telling her, "We are going to do something important together!"

To Robin who supported the project by letting me and Melanie use her home as a work space.

To Katie Plax who gave me the idea for the title.

To Colin and Cameron Jones who connected me to their former professor, Carl Nordgren.

And to Carl who first connected me to Torchflame Publishing.

Deepest acknowledgements go to Teri Rider, my publisher. She expressed immediate support and understanding of this project. She gave a voice to that three-year-old child inside of me that didn't have one for so very long ago. Teri also gave voice to my beloved little sister, Betsy, and the many, many other children who are now silent and will never have a chance to tell their story.

Lastly, I wish to thank that barber who cut my hair

sixty-four years ago. He will never know the depth to which his kind words sustained me and gave me strength. Though I never had a chance to thank him personally, I do so with the Kindness Project—simple acts that bring a smile and touch a heart—that my granddaughter, Eleanor, and I co-founded.

Please never underestimate the power of an act that honors a person's value. It can truly save a life.

About the Authors

Photo Credit: Harry Bradley

With more than 30 years of experience as a therapist, Connie has shared her expertise and her somatic, heart-centered approach with countless adults and young people, helping them to understand and address trauma and its impact on their lives.

Throughout her career, Connie has done television interviews, trainings, talks, and presentations to hospitals, youth groups, and other organizations. Connie has been committed to sharing the psychological — and the physical and spiritual aspects to overcoming traumatic experiences. *Green Glitter Girl*, her debut book, delves deeper into the approach. Her own journey of healing after trauma informs her work as a therapist; she is passionate about helping others find a way to bring peace and wellbeing to their own lives. Connie was interviewed for the book, The Forever Angels by P.M.H. Atwater, L.H.D., published in 2019.

Connie is married (Harry) and lives in St. Louis, MO. She has a son (Bobby) and a daughter (Sarah) and four grandchildren. Recently she and her granddaughter, Eleanor were recently featured on KMOV in St. Louis for their heartfelt efforts, The Kindness Project.

Photo Credit: Kaitlin Parry

Co-author Melanie Davis-Jones holds a degree in English from Duke University. An experienced brand strategist and nonprofit executive, she serves on the board of Soul Seeds, a nonprofit organization that supports the social-emotional health of individuals in underserved communities by teaching specific meditation techniques. Her passion for service was fueled by fifteen years as a volunteer with Source Force, a small grassroots group that provided meals, clothing, groceries, and love to people with HIV/AIDS. Melanie lives in Los Angeles, CA and has identical twin sons (Cameron and Colin). She is a skilled intuitive energy healer, certified in trauma-informed approaches, with a private practice, Zaia Energy Works.

Thank You!

Thank you for reading! If you enjoyed this book, please leave a review on Amazon, Goodreads, BookBub, The Story Graph, or anywhere else you like to track your recent reads. Alternatively, you could post online or tell a friend about it. This helps our authors more than you may know.

   - The Team at Torchflame Books

Follow Torchflame Books for news about our authors and upcoming new releases @TorchflameBooks.

Find your next great read at www.torchflamebooks.com.